277 Secrets Your Dog
Wants You to Know

277 SECRETS YOUR DOG WANTS YOU TO KNOW

A Doggie Bag
of Unusual and Useful
Information

Paulette Cooper
and
Paul Noble

TEN SPEED PRESS

1🅢

Ten Speed Press
P.O. Box 7123
Berkeley, California 94707

Cover design by Paulette Cooper, Norma Hirsch, and Gail Belenson
Cover photograph courtesy Rex USA Ltd.
Interior illustrations by Ellen Joy Sasaki, except on pages
1, 48, 60, 67, 70, 117, 136, 138, 149, 158, and 175

Cooper, Paulette.
  277 secrets your dog wants you to know: a doggie bag of unusual and useful information / Paulette Cooper and Paul Noble.
    p.   cm.
  Includes bibliographical references and index.
  ISBN 0-89815-737-4 (9hc)
  ISBN 0-89815-682-3 (pbk.)
    1. Dogs--Miscellanea.   I. Noble, Paul (Paul R.)   II. Title.
SF426.C67 1995
    636.7--dc20   94-46971
                                                                        CIP

Library of Congress Cataloging-in-Publication Data

Printed in Canada.

9 10 — 99 98 97

To our best friends who are no longer with us

Pom Pom

Yo Yo

Tiki

Wags

Contents

Acknowledgments

We are very grateful to the following people who allowed us to interview them for this book. (A listing of all *written* sources is contained in the back.) We especially wish to thank Herbert Salm, D.V.M., of Greenwich, Connecticut, who "vetted" this book for us, and attorney Albert Podell, Esq.,our friend and a former editor, who has improved our lives and our books.

Cleveland Amory; Father John Andrew; Leigh Applebrook; Jeff Ashley; Barbara Austin; Michelle Bamberger, D.V.M.; Anmarie Barrie, Esq.; Ross Becker; Carol Lea Benjamin; Barbara Bouyet; Robert Brown, D.V.M.; Bud Brownhill; Roger Caras; Sherry Carpenter; Rabbi Neil Cooper; J. Michael Cornwell, D.V.M.; Kendall Crolius; Abe Eastwood, Ph.D.; Warren Eckstein; Jay Empel, D.V.M.; Sally Fekety; William Fortney, D.V.M.; Lisa Gilford; Gary Goin; Richard Greene, D.V.M.; Wayne Grover; Captain Arthur J. Haggerty; Monsignor Thomas Hartman; Katherine Haupt, V.M.D., Ph.D.; Guy Hodge; Gwen Ivy, Ph.D.; Elayne Kahn, Ph.D., Al-Haaj Ghazi Khankan; Brian Kilcommons; Amy Marder, V.M.D.; Bern Markowitz; Dennis Marks; Gayle Martz; Molly McGuire; Nicole Mezo; Bill Milgram, Ph.D.; James Miller, D.V.M.; Dee Newhall; Reverend Julie Parker; Florence Phillips; Ernest Poortinga, D.V.M.; Steven Radbill, D.V.M.; Mary Randolph, Esq.; Joel Rapp; Gayle Roberts, D.V.M.; Margot Rosenberg; Susan Hall Sheehan; Mordecai Siegal; Irwin Small, D.V.M.; Scott S. Smith; John Walsh; George Whitney, D.V.M.; and Steve Willett.

In addition, we wish to thank the people who didn't want to be named: the three flight attendants, and those who responded to our ad seeking information from dog owners who had lost their dogs and been scammed afterwards. We also thank all the people we interviewed for the chapters on offbeat or life-saving products for dogs.

We also wish to thank the following veterinary colleges for responding to our requests for information: Colorado State University, Kansas State University, Louisiana State University, Purdue University, Texas A&M University, Tuskegee University, and the University of Illinois.

We are also grateful to the librarians at the American Kennel Club for the use of their extensive library on dogs.

The hundreds of written sources we consulted are included in Suggested Reading (and Viewing) About Dogs, which is at the end of the book. Many acknowledgments are also interspersed within the body of the book; as authors ourselves, we tried wherever possible to mention the names of other authors' relevant books.

Introduction

Reading this book will make you your dog's best friend! Never before has one pet book covered so many subjects and presented so many secrets and tips. Most cover only one subject, such as health, breed, or behavior. But what follows is a veritable pet-pourri of information in dozens of areas of interest to the dog lover.

Our goal was to write a book which would appeal to dog nuts like us. Since our attention span isn't much longer than our dogs', that meant writing a book which would contain many short, easy-to-read articles on a variety of interesting topics for people who want to bone up on dogs.

Most of these subjects—and secrets—have never appeared in a dog book before. A few have, but were buried in a paragraph or on a page of the 6,000 books that have been written about, for—and even by—dogs. Not only will this material probably be new to you, but it is presented differently, so that it will be more relevant to your dog and your life.

We found that too many dog books asked provocative questions about dogs, and then answered with discussions of the authors' dogs, or those they knew, trained, handled, observed, or analyzed. Even though we both have advanced degrees, in psychology or communications, we didn't think you wanted to know what *we* knew about dogs, but rather what *experts* knew. We also suspected that you don't want to read about *our* dogs, but rather what would help *your* dogs. So we didn't even mention our dogs (Pinki and Pucci) in this book, except one time, when we got carried away. (Sorry, we couldn't help ourselves.)

Thus, you are about to read approximately 125 chapters and side-bars, which we call "sidebarks," based on over fifty interviews and hundreds of books and newspaper, newsletter, and journal articles from the past five years. A few of the people we interviewed will be familiar to dog lovers, such as Cleveland Amory, Carol Lea Benjamin, Roger Caras, Sherry Carpenter, Warren Eckstein, Captain Haggerty, Brian Kilcommons, Mordecai Siegal, and others.

They, along with veterinarians, scientists, behaviorists, trainers, and a large number of experts you may not have heard of, will present you with a doglopedia of secrets, findings, ideas, suggestions, thoughts, and tips on how your dogs can live longer, healthier, happier, and safer lives so you can enjoy yours for many more years.

In the following pages, you'll learn how to understand what your dogs are trying to tell you so you can communicate with them better; how to show them off so you can share them with others; how to teach them a few simple things so they behave better; how you can be even happier with them—and vice versa; what to buy for them; what to read about them; along with much, much more.

We included more "controversial" and "negative" material than one usually finds in dog books, so some of this information may make you slightly uncomfortable. Like the possible connection between dogs and multiple sclerosis, or little-known dangers that could kill your dogs.

We felt that you should know about these things for your own sake as well as your pet's. Dogs are a gigantic responsibility; the more you know, the more you can truly be their best friends. If you're not informed and something happens, not only will you have needlessly hurt your pals, but your grief will be compounded by guilt that comes from knowing you could have prevented their illness or death.

We also do a little more moralizing and include more material on socially relevant dog issues than one might expect to find in a book of information. But we didn't want to just write facts. We hoped to make the dog-owning public aware of some of the problems out there, such as the dreadful things we do to dogs in this world. After all, if dog lovers don't know or care what's going on, no other segment of the population is going to do anything about these situations.

Before we begin, we want to apologize for using the word "he" whenever we refer to dogs in this book. It isn't personal; both our teacup Shih Tzus are females. But alternating between "he" and "she" is awkward, we didn't want to refer to a dog as "it," and, like it or not, in our language we have a tendency to refer to dogs as "he" and cats as "she."

Finally, most of the people we interviewed are thanked in the acknowledgments, and the written sources are recognized in Suggested Reading (and Viewing) About Dogs, which is at the end of the book. We also wish to thank our agent, Ted Chichak, for his unflagging support and enthusiasm, and our editor, Lorena Jones.

Especially, though, we want to thank Phil Wood and Jo Ann Deck of Ten Speed Press. We always considered it a delight to be their friends; now we're honored to be their authors, too.

Is It Safe to Let Your Dog "Kiss" Your Face—and Should You Let Him Lick Your Feet?

Letting your dog "kiss" you will probably not harm you; indeed, the danger may be greater to him than to you! But beware: what you might catch is rather surprising—and what your dog could contract is even more astonishing.

But don't worry too much if you've got a dog who likes to leap and love and lick you. "I don't think it can ever be suggested that letting your dog lick your face is a *good* idea, but I can't say a lot of diseases are commonly transmitted that way," says James B. Miller, D.V.M., who has written about zoonotic (shared by animal and man) diseases.

"Obviously, it's not really a sanitary thing to do," this professor of internal medicine adds. For example, dogs do sniff other dogs' fecal matter, "but you probably won't get anything from that particular bacteria," he hastens to state.

Dr. Miller points out that "although dogs' mouths *do* have a lot of bacteria, the amount of bacteria that goes through our mouths every day is astronomical. We're constantly touching our mouths and faces and handling all kinds of things. The question is whether these bacteria are going to cause problems."

This professor from the Atlantic Veterinary College at the University of Prince Edward Island in Canada concedes that most of the time the bacteria dogs may introduce don't cause difficulties. That is, unless the person has an open sore or a wound on his or her face, or anyplace else on his or her body, for that matter.

Incredibly, some people believe that letting a dog lick their wound speeds healing. It doesn't. "You can get an infection because of the bacteria in a dog's mouth," Dr. Miller warns.

So, if you don't have an open sore, are not immune-deficient (in which case you're more likely to catch something), and you or your

Go Ahead and Treat Your Dog Like a Baby

To spoil or not to spoil a dog has long been a bone of contention among many. But one study shows that it won't make your dog behave any worse if you indulge him and treat him like a member of the family. In fact, it may even make him behave *better*.

A study of 730 people conducted at the Veterinary Hospital of the University of Pennsylvania and Mercer University in Georgia, examined the consequences of treating dogs like small humans with fur.

Dog owners answered questions about whether they let their dogs sleep on their beds, get on furniture, share snacks with them, whether they confided in them, took them on errands, celebrated their birthdays, bought them clothes and unlimited treats, or engaged in other indulgent or anthropomorphic behavior.

What happened to the dogs? Nothing. According to the study, published in *Applied Animal Behaviour Science* (vol. 34, 1992), those who "spoiled" their dogs were no more likely to report that their dogs engaged in problem behavior (vocalization, destruction, running away, disobedience, fearful behaviors, refusal to listen, and aggression) than those who did not.

In fact, dogs who were taken on trips, and who shared snacks or received food from the table were significantly *less* likely to display negative behavior.

---

dog is not sick (when you should be more cautious in general), can you catch *anything* by having your dog lick your face?

Yes, and the most surprising malady is cat scratch disease! "Dogs have been shown to occasionally transmit cat scratch disease," Dr. Miller says. "They don't ever get sick from it themselves, but they can be carriers."

Although the name sounds innocuous enough, it's a potentially disabling disease. Furthermore, it causes enlargement of the lymph glands, which can be misdiagnosed as cancer of the lymph nodes.

A far more common ailment you might get from your dog, though, is strep throat. Vets have reported recurring cases of strep throat in families that have dogs and children who trade kisses back and forth.

The Real Reasons Dogs Lick Us

Some cynics say dogs only lick us because they like the salt on our skin. Indeed, some support for this comes from a recent study done at Hokkaido University in Sapporo, Japan, which was reported in *Cornell University Animal Health Newsletter*. The study found that dogs really do like salt, partly because it can enhance their taste responses.

Fine, but dogs also lick other dogs, and we know it's not because salt is involved. These licks on the nose and mouth may be a form of greeting. Or they may help them recognize the scent on the other dogs. And puppies also lick their mothers' faces, soliciting food from them in this manner.

So, maybe dogs lick us for all the above reasons. We are their parents, their friends, their packmates—and they love us not just because we're so sweet, but because we're so salty.

But in general, face-licking is probably far riskier for a dog than for his owner—because he could catch tuberculosis from it! And since people don't always know they have TB, "they can transmit it to their dogs without realizing it," notes Dr. Miller, who adds, "There have been no reports of dogs transmitting it to humans."

Tuberculosis in dogs is an increasing problem. "There appears to be an increased prevalence of dogs with tuberculosis in North America just as there are now more people with TB. A sick person coughs and has sputum on his lip, and then the dog kisses or licks his mouth. Or the person coughs into a tissue, which falls to the floor, and the dog chews it."

Finally, more for the children's benefit than for the dogs', Dr. Miller asked us to add that he doesn't think it's the best idea to have dogs licking *children's* faces.

Not all veterinarians agree that it's all right for all dogs to lick any of our faces. Steven Radbill, D.V.M., believes that with certain dogs, "It's not that you *shouldn't* let them kiss you, but you should be aware that there is a potential problem." He says it can occur with dogs who have what he calls a "smushed-in" face, like Sharpeis, pugs, or Boston terriers. These dogs, he says, "have a tendency to get pseudomonas infections in their lip folds, and people can catch it from them. I have one client who won't stop kissing her dog and she has gotten it several times."

The doctor, who also owns the Radbill Animal Hospital in Philadelphia, says, "You can protect yourself by checking before you let your dog kiss you to see if your dog's face emits a strong smell, which indicates he may have this infection." Incidentally, to stop a dog from kissing your face (or your child's), dog trainer Bashkim Dibra suggests you blow into his face and firmly say "no" when he tries to lick you.

You may also be wondering if it's safe for your dog to lick your eyes. "Certain bacteria occasionally could cause a conjunctivitis or something," says Dr. Miller. "But bacteria get in our eyes all the time and our normal tear secretions help clean them and prevent infections."

Finally, one veterinarian warns about letting dogs lick the other end of our bodies—our feet. "Athlete's foot is caused by different organisms. There have been some interesting cases in the literature where people with the fungus have let their dogs lick their feet and then the dog has gotten that fungus on its face," Dr. George D. Whitney, a retired veterinarian from Connecticut, told us.

Embarrassing Habits of Your Dog (You've Been Ashamed to Ask Anyone About)

Dave Barry once wrote that we think so highly of dogs that we hardly even notice that "they spend the bulk of their free time circling around with other dogs to see which one can sniff the other the most times in the crotch."

Dogs do have some habits that to us may seem disgusting, embarrassing—or both. Here, according to some top animal behaviorists, is why they do them, and what you can do about them.

My dog passes some truly horrendous gas. What can I do?

Leave the room. Seriously, gas can be caused by foods high in protein or cellulose, or by a food allergy. It's especially likely to occur in older dogs because of their slowed intestinal function.

Flatulence may also occur if a dog eats only once a day. That can cause him to become ravenous and gulp down food, swallowing air in the process, believes well-known animal expert Dr. Michael Fox. His suggestions are to feed your dog more often, and experiment with foods.

You can also try crumbling charcoal pills onto the dog's food weekly, or a new product called Curtail. It's produced by the same company that makes Beano, which reduces gas in people. Curtail supposedly does the same for dogs.

Note: if this problem is very pronounced and accompanied by other symptoms, especially digestive upsets, it could be serious and require immediate veterinary attention.

My dog will find something like bird droppings on the street and roll around in it in ecstasy. It's embarrassing if there's anyone around. Why does he do this?

Dogs sometimes cheerfully throw themselves down on decaying bird droppings, cow or horse manure, rotting garbage, and other odiferous fare. Some believe their euphoria may be an instinctual response established many generations ago, when the strong smell generally meant they had just come upon the dung of some species that was hunting nearby.

They may then roll around in it or "self-scent" to camouflage their own odor, and perhaps make themselves smell more like what they're chasing.

In *Dogwatching*, Desmond Morris also points out that if a dog rolls around in the dung of another species and returns to join other dogs, he is then "telling" them what he found and possibly instigating a group hunt.

My dog sniffs stool from other dogs and even tries to eat it. What can I do?

Dogs smell other dogs' stool as a way of learning about them. When dogs defecate, small anal glands on either side of the rectum add a strong-smelling substance to the feces. Bruce Fogle, D.V.M., M.R.C.V.S., says that for the other dogs, these droppings are like "reading newspapers, only better." From the stool, a dog can tell the sex of the dog who left it; and if it's a male, how "masculine" he is; if a female, whether she's coming into season, or is in heat now.

As for ingesting stool, although it's disgusting to us, puppies often eat their first droppings. Dr. Fogle writes in *101 Questions Your Dog Would Ask Its Vet* that dogs may revert to this early coprophagy when they grow up because of a lack of digestive enzymes. He recommends feeding dogs enzyme-containing foods, like pineapple, pumpkin, or papaya fruit.

You can also buy a product like Forbid (available through Wholesale Pet USA), to sprinkle onto your dog's food to make feces less appealing. Others suggest putting red pepper sauce on the droppings so your dog will be repelled and avoid eating feces in the future.

My male keeps lifting his leg even after there is no urine left. Is he trying to show off or something?

No, he's really showing off his heredity. Sex hormones are excreted in the urine, and some say a male dog lifts his leg and urinates sideways to make these hormones more accessible to other dogs.

Do Dogs Get VD?

The question was asked and answered by Ann L. Huntington, D.V.M., who writes an engrossing pets column that appears in newspapers throughout the country. She said that dogs *can* get VD—two types, in fact. They can also get it the same way people do—through promiscuity.

The first and rarer kind, transmissible venereal tumors, are "large wart-like growths on the genitalia that are spread through sexual intercourse," she writes. Dr. Steven Radbill says, "It's found mainly in stray dog populations, and if untreated, can lead to cancer. To guard against this, don't let your dog roam and breed indiscriminately."

The other form of VD is brucellosis, the bane of the breeder. It's highly contagious, causing many bitches to abort and males to become sterile. The Merck Veterinary Manual says that "transmission is congenital, venereal, or by ingestion of contaminated materials. All ages and both sexes appear to be equally susceptible." According to *Canine News*, as many as one in ten dogs carry *B. canis*, which can be transmitted to humans, for example, by handling aborted fetuses from female dogs with the disease.

They then "read" his odor messages, and leave their own scent marks. So your dog may just be trying to leave a message, not show off how many times he can write out that message. Still, by aiming high, some think he may be hinting that he's large and macho.

Lifting his leg may also have a practical purpose. Desmond Morris indicates that urinating higher up may keep the scent signals fresher than on the ground, where they'd be disturbed. It also brings the scent stains up to the nose level of other dogs, making your dog more conspicuous, and his scent more accessible.

Why does my male dog insist on grabbing my leg and thrusting against it at the most embarrassing times, like when our minister is visiting? And what can we do about it?

One reason dogs hump human legs is that they may be extremely frustrated. Although we're horrified and embarrassed by it, they don't consider it wrong because they simply view us as part of their pack.

Many adult male dogs try to mount legs because they're sexually frustrated. Female dogs are only in heat a couple of times a year, and male dogs may not be able to do anything about it then either. So some dogs will mount anything standing or lying still, including cats, other male dogs, cushions, and, yes, human legs, which are easy for them to get their own legs around. In addition to it being a substitute sexual activity, mounting is also a sign of dominance, a behavior pattern developed as a puppy, and often reverted to when the older dog becomes excited.

Picking your dog up and putting him on your lap to stop him, or making a big deal out of the mounting gives him extra attention and therefore generally does not extinguish the behavior. Some dog experts advocate hormones, or castration, but the latter may not work if the habit was well established before the dog was desexed, say behaviorists David Ross and Ruth Weston in *Dog Problems*.

Other ways to stop the mounting are by diverting them in some way, such as spraying a noxious substance, or lifting your knee to a large dog's chest. For long-term solutions, there's obedience training, behavior modification, and nonphysical discipline techniques.

Isolation is also commonly suggested, that is, putting the dog in a quiet room for a few minutes each time he tries to mount. But be warned! Fogle wrote of a "salacious dachshund" who had to be isolated eighty-four times the first day this technique was used. But three weeks later, the dog was no longer mounting.

My dog sometimes sniffs me in embarrassing areas. Why?

Dr. Peter Neville, a top English consultant in animal behavior, writes in *Pet Sex* that "it's all very natural" for dogs to "head for an area where there's lots of scent information to be gleaned. It's like shaking hands in a world that we have so little sensory awareness of…. They do things which are natural for them, no matter how rude they may be for us."

My dog has breath that could knock the Statue of Liberty off her perch. Why, and what can I do?

Dogs smell of the food they eat; if they eat manure or fish they'll smell like it. But Dr. Fogle says problem smells can also come from the stomach. So if your dog has room-clearing breath, try changing his diet.

Commonly, though, bad breath comes from bad teeth and gum problems. So have his teeth cleaned annually by your veterinarian; keep up his daily brushing, if possible. You might try some of the many products sold to improve dogs' breath, even though that only masks the problem.

Am I imagining things, or is our female dog coming onto my husband?

Female dogs can be nymphomaniacs as a result of hormone production. But even female dogs with normal hormone levels may flirt—especially with men—when they come into heat. Dr. Neville writes that the female dog "may solicit her human family, and other people, often men, with a rear-end waggle."

"New" Pill May Stop
Your Dog from Aging

A drug called l-deprenyl has shown amazing success with diminishing the symptoms of aging in dogs—and it may soon add years to your dog's life as well.

If you've ever had an older dog, you've seen that as dogs start to age, some lose interest in food; fail to recognize their surroundings; develop dysfunctions in sleep, attention and activities; forget their house-training; stop responding to commands; lose their hearing; vocalize inappropriately (like barking or whining when they shouldn't); have difficulties in climbing stairs and being alone; exhibit compulsive behavior such as circling; and suffer from tremors, arthritic stiffness, and/or weakness.

"This decline starts in dogs at around eight," says Dr. Bill Milgram, a professor of psychology and neurophysiology at the University of Toronto. (Depressingly, Milgram says the mental deterioration starts in humans at around fifty to fifty-five!)

L-deprenyl, in one study, improved almost all cognitive aging problems mentioned above except in two areas: whining, and tolerance to being left alone. This study was abstracted in the *Applied Animal Behaviour Science* (volume 39 [2], February, 1994).

One veterinarian who participated in one of the trials used his own fifteen-year-old poodle, who had become so confused it couldn't remember how to get back in his house from outside. After two to three weeks on deprenyl, the dog showed a significant reduction in geriatric symptoms, stated an article in *Veterinary Product News* (July/August, 1993).

Several studies of l-deprenyl on rats have also been quite dramatic, and deprenyl-fed rats have lived considerably longer than controls. In one study, reported in *Life Sciences* (volume 45 [6] 1989), deprenyl kept "alive a male rat population beyond the maximum age

Your Dog's "Arthritis" May Be Ingrown Toenails!

Lameness that might appear to be a result of arthritis, could actually arise from too-long or ingrown toenails, according to a report in *Bottom Line*. Since older dogs are less active than younger ones, they may not get enough exercise to wear down their nails naturally. The untrimmed nails then continue to grow, curling and twisting, sometimes even growing into a pad of the paw.

A quick visual check of your dog's paws may uncover a simple solution to what you thought was a debilitating problem.

of death (182 weeks)," which they called "unprecedented." Indeed, one of the rats lived to 224 weeks, while the longest living rat in the control group lived only 164 weeks.

Could deprenyl also help dogs to live longer? "One might assume that since it increases the longevity of rats, it would also do the same for dogs since their metabolisms aren't that different," says Dr. Gwen Ivy, an expert in aging, and an associate professor of psychology and anatomy/cell biology at the University of Toronto.

As for whether deprenyl might one day be used to prolong *people's* lives, Dr. Ivy believes that it *might* increase our life span because it appears to promote the production of free radical scavengers, and increases their levels in the brain.

A Kansas-based company, Deprenyl Animal Health, Inc., in Overland Park, partially owned by Draxis Health Inc., near Toronto, is the one who will soon be marketing the drug. Since deprenyl affects dopamine production in the brain, it is currently being used by some medical doctors to treat Parkinson's disease.

Most veterinarians, however, have not heard of this pill. That will probably change soon. Deprenyl, if and when approved for dogs by the FDA, will be marketed under the trade name Anipryl.

Dr. Milgram, whose studies have also demonstrated cognitive improvement of dogs given deprenyl, admonishes that it didn't have any effect on young or normal healthy dogs. "But if I had a really old dog with problems I would try it," he says.

Dirty Tricks at Dog Shows

Someone is killing the great dogs of England! In a May 15, 1994, story published by the Times Newspapers Ltd., it was revealed that there have been a series of attacks on—and murders of—champion pedigree dogs. These assaults appear to have been carried out by rivals, who have been poisoning competitive dogs with hallucinogenic drugs, tranquilizers, and rat killers.

According to the story by Ian Burrell, nine show dogs have been poisoned during the past two years in England. Five of them have died. These include a rottweiler who was fed a rat-poison cocktail, and a champion puli who died from internal bleeding after consuming an ecstasy-type drug. Another puli needed several days of treatment after acid was sprayed on his back.

The article also revealed that dogs have been sprayed with dye, painted with nail polish, and had clumps of hair cut out of their coats. Additionally, high-frequency dog alarms, inaudible to the human ear and used for subduing aggressive dogs, have been secretly set off to distract champions as they paraded before the judges.

Who is doing this? According to Beverly Cuddy, editor of *Dogs Today* magazine, "You think [of people who show dogs as]… nice little old ladies wearing tweed suits—but there is a nasty element too." This element no doubt has some relation to the fact that winning animals are worth tens of thousands of dollars when sold to foreign buyers. And the owners of champions, like the winner of the Crufts Dog Show (England's equivalent of Westminster), might make up to £75,000 the following year advertising pet foods and accessories.

Surprisingly, it may be the Americans who behave better at dog shows. While we may be the ones with guns, at least we're not literally shooting down the competition. Except when drugs are concerned. In California, a fifteen-thousand-dollar price tag was put on

Your Dog Could Make You a Crime Victim

We sometimes let our guard down in situations involving dogs, thinking that anyone approaching us in such matters has to be a caring, altruistic person. Criminals, knowing we're more trusting where dogs are concerned, have taken advantage of it. For example:

- Two women in California were raped when they let men into their house to see puppies they had advertised to sell.

- People have been robbed when bringing cash to pay rewards to those who falsely claimed they found their lost dog.

- The home of a wealthy couple in Arizona was burglarized when they went to pick up their stolen dog—who turned out to have been kidnapped just to get the couple to leave their house.

Always exercise reasonable caution where your pets are concerned, just as you would in any situation these days.

the head of a drug-sniffing dog who was responsible for more than a hundred arrests. Someone made sure there wouldn't be any more, because the dog was mysteriously murdered.

Mostly, though, nastiness among American dog showers was described by show judge Walter Goodman to *USA Today* as "sort of like a Tonya Harding thing." That makes it sound like those who show dogs here are going around bashing the competitors' dogs in the kneecaps. But all that's happening is that some owners use black shoe polish, felt-tip pens, or eye liner to make a dog's coat or nose look blacker, according to an exposé in *Dog World*, by Cle Francis.

Although there's supposed to be no foreign substances on the dog, owners may also use a paste of peroxide and milk of magnesia to get the pink fluid out of their eyes. Or laundry bleach or cornstarch to make the coat whiter or softer. Or hair spray to make the coat stand out.

Francis also revealed that an owner might "accidentally" step on a competing show dog's paw, or the back of its handler's shoe. Or the owner might secretly give the dog a dye job. But considering that "dye job" in England seems to mean "die job," perhaps Americans are not that uncivilized after all.

A Dog's Eye View of Obedience Class

The author of the following amusing article is unknown, although it purports to be written by a dog.

The [obedience] tests...will bore you to death, but with your own variations you can play forever and score your own way:

- HEEL ON LEAD: ...Walk as slowly as you can, then spring forward with all your weight. If your handler falls flat on his face, you score 25 points.

- RECALL: When [your handler] shouts at you, assume rock deafness.... On no account sit in front of your handler, because he will only make you heel....25 points if handler loses voice.

- RETRIEVE THE DUMBBELL: ...On no account fetch it back, because he will only throw it away again. If he wants the stupid piece of wood let him fetch it himself; you will be help- ing to train him not to throw away things he really wants.... You get 5 points every time handler gets dumbbell.

- SIT: ...Stay one inch away from the ground at the back end.

- CONCLUSION: ...Do any exercise you choose perfectly! This will leave your handler thinking that the earlier mistakes were his fault, and he will take you to training classes week after week.

The above first appeared in a newsletter called *Rott 'N Chatter*, pub- lished by Jan Cooper of Anaheim, California. It was then reprinted by *Canine Classified* in Houston.

Do Dogs Cause Multiple Sclerosis?

Ask just about any veterinarian or medical doctor if there's a connection between dogs and multiple sclerosis and they always deny it. But several articles and letters have appeared in prestigious medical journals, stating that there is a significant association between distemper epidemics in dogs and a subsequent rise in cases of multiple sclerosis.

Naturally, because two events follow in time does not mean that there is a definite cause-and-effect relationship. But there have been a number of intriguing correlations in many places that are hard to ignore.

Unfortunately, the top researcher in the field, Stuart D. Cook, M.D., at the Department of Neurosciences at the New Jersey Medical School in Newark, declined to be interviewed for this book. But his papers speak clearly enough.

In his first article, published in *The Lancet* on May 7, 1977, Dr. Cook and a co-researcher found significantly more small indoor dogs belonging to a group of MS sufferers as compared with controls. (Twenty-six small dogs belonging to twenty-nine MS subjects versus sixteen of twenty-nine in the control group.)

His later articles focused less on the size of the dogs and more on whether they had ever suffered from distemper. Indeed, this article described one family with four sisters, three of whom had MS. The sister with neurological symptoms left home in 1971. Afterwards, the three remaining sisters had close contact with an aged family dog, who developed a distemper-like disease in 1973. At various times in 1974, all three sisters showed their first symptoms of MS.

Dr. Cook and his colleagues later studied a cluster of multiple sclerosis cases that occurred in Key West, Florida, from 1977 to 1983. In their letter, published in *The Lancet* on June 20, 1987, they pointed out that most of the MS patients worked or lived in or near Stock

Island, a poor neighborhood, where there were many stray and unvaccinated dogs. From anecdotal reports, Cook learned of a high rate of distemper in this area between 1969 and the mid-1970s.

But this letter never mentioned some other potentially relevant factors. We examined a few articles that appeared on the subject in the *Miami Herald* from 1985 through 1988. They also reported that almost all of those with MS had some association to Stock Island. And they brought out one odd connection between the MS patients, which was not where they lived but how they worked.

Of the approximately twenty-nine patients, there were eight diagnosed cases of *nurses* with MS, plus two medical technicians—and all worked at the same Key West hospital. It may also be relevant then that prior to the epidemic, Key West dumped its raw sewage near its drinking water.

Additionally, in Stock Island, there was a huge 19-acre, 6-story city dump, referred to unaffectionately by the citizens as "Mount Trashmore." As the *Miami Herald* noted, "Mercury leaches from the dump into nearby ocean sediments. Flocks of gulls feast there and scatter droppings...."

Of course birds are not the only ones to disseminate toxins, etc. Perhaps dogs congregated at the dump as well, and then went elsewhere in Stock Island, possibly explaining a canine connection to the disease, if there was one.

In other letters and papers, Dr. Cook and his colleagues also present time links between CDV (canine distemper virus) and MS in other locations, specifically in the Faroe islands; in Sitka, Alaska; in the Orkney and Shetland islands near Scotland; and in Iceland. But most others have been unable to confirm this, questioning Dr. Cook's method, as well as his interpretation and analysis.

Still, several researchers working independently claim to have found correlations between MS and distemper in Germany, Newfoundland, and Scandinavia as recently as 1993. But other researchers have also failed to support this.

The debate rages. Here are some of the issues:

- Are small dogs more likely to be a factor—if indeed

dogs are a factor at all—in the transmission of the disease, or are they simply more likely to be kept indoors and therefore are in closer contact with their owners?

- Is there one virus or are there many?
- Is the disease contagious?
- If there is a connection, between contact with dogs that have distemper and the onset of multiple sclerosis, how many years does it take to develop?
- Does environmental exposure play a role?
- If the development of MS involves the transmission of a virus (like CDV) from animal to man, why has the virus never been found in an MS patient?

At present there are no answers to these questions, or to the main one: is there a causal relationship between canine distemper and multiple sclerosis? The question of whether canine distemper is associated with human diseases first appeared in the medical literature in 1928 and it may go on for many more years before an answer is found, if ever.

Until anyone knows something definitive, the best thing might be for you to cover all your bases and take some precautions. Whenever you're around any sick dog, wash your hands after handling him, and be careful about letting him lick you.

As for distemper, a highly contagious and usually fatal viral disease in dogs, the early signs are fever, coughing, sneezing, runny eyes and nose, vomiting, diarrhea, loss of appetite, and generalized malaise. In the final stages, it attacks the dog's nervous system and can cause seizures, etc.

The only way to tell for sure if a dog has distemper is to test his blood or tissues. The important thing is to make it unnecessary by keeping up his vaccinations. After all, the life you save may be your dog's.

We asked the director of the Research Grant Program for the National Multiple Sclerosis Society, Abe Eastwood, Ph.D., to comment on the possible relationship between MS and distemper in dogs.

"As far as I know," he said, "the evidence isn't very good and I think most people don't agree with Dr. Cook, who is the main advocate of the theory.

"There's no evidence that a virus is directly involved in causing MS," he continued. "We know that it's an autoimmune disease, and that the immune system for some reason mistakenly attacks part of the person's body. We know that at least part of the reason that it does that is genetic, and there's good reason to suspect that something in the environment triggers that attack but we don't know what that is."

Could it be a virus? "Several studies indicated that the symptoms of MS often get worse after an upper respiratory viral infection, but that's no indication that it's a direct result of a virus. People have searched very hard for a virus but no one has ever identified one that seems to have any relation to MS."

21 Spots Your Dog Loves to Have Scratched, Tickled, Touched, Petted, Rubbed, or Massaged

If you find a spot your dog likes to have touched, he'll be the first to let you know. "He'll look at you like 'don't stop,' or get a hypnotic look like 'that was really good, I want more.' He may lick you, fall asleep, sigh, push his body toward you or your hand toward him to encourage you to do more, blink his eyes, make a strange happy throat-scratching sound," says Nicole Mezo, a certified massage therapist in Mill Valley, California, who also massages dogs, and is the author of *On Cloud K-9: How to Massage Your Dog.*

To find out what dogs like best, we interviewed her, along with others who do occasional pet massages, like Leigh Applebrook of The Pet Department Store in New York, and massage therapists, Lisa Corwin and Fanny Mandelberger.

Don't try any of the following on dogs you don't know well, however, and start out cautiously even on your own dog. He may be overly sensitive in some areas and react unpredictably. Tufts University's School of Veterinary Medicine's *Your Dog* newsletter cautions against massaging areas "near fractures, sprains, or ruptured vertebral disks," along with inflamed swollen or bruised areas.

If you massage any one of the first three regions below, your dog will be especially happy because you'll be doing for him what he can't do for himself.

1. **Gums:** A dog may have a mild irritation and sore spots in his mouth area, which may be why you see him rubbing the sides of his head against the floor or hard edges of furniture. Or it may be his ears!

   But if his teeth are the problem, you'll help him get relief if you rub your fingers along his lower gum line. Not under his chin; just gently below the outline of his teeth, over the fur. (Be careful since some dogs bite if you approach the mouth area.)

Robert Browning Loved Elizabeth Barrett Browning, but Not Her Dog

"Grow old along with me—but not unless you get rid of that ★&@#%★ dog!" is what poet Robert Browning might have written. But Elizabeth Barrett's dog almost had the last bark by nearly preventing one of the most famous romances in history.

Flush, her cocker spaniel, knew something was afoot the first time Browning called on Elizabeth, and he tried to nip the romance in the bud by biting Browning on the ankle.

But Browning refused to admit de-feet. The first time Flush was kidnapped by a ring of dog thieves—which was common in those days and explains why he was abducted two more times—he refused to pay the ransom. Elizabeth paid it, the romance flourished, and Flush ultimately went along on their honeymoon, according to writer Lorna Powers.

Incidentally, if his gum line seems very sore, or you note a lot of odor or swelling, your dog needs more than a rub. He needs a trip to the vet.

2. **In front of his ears:** Dogs often have problems with wax, fluids, foreign objects, and mites in their ear canals. Since they can't stick their paws into their ears, they may get some relief when you gently rub that area from the outside.

3. **Below the ears, near the jaw**: Move your fingers an inch or two down the ears toward the jaw, gently, because your dog may experience some discomfort. In addition, the salivary and lymph glands are in this region and they can be very sensitive to touch.

The following areas are stimulating to a dog—sometimes overly so. Puppies, for example, when handled between the front legs may try to mount your arm. If you're already having troubles like your dog mounting, you may not want to excite your dog any further and may choose to skip some of these spots.

4. **The chest:** Pet behaviorist Barbara Woodhouse says that a dog will become almost hypnotized if you gently tickle his chest, between his front legs, with your palms up, facing him. Touch-

ing this area is particularly exciting to dogs, whose chests are stimulated when they mount other dogs.

5. **The groin:** Many people go out of their way not to touch a dog in this region—but many knowledgeable animal experts encourage the opposite. The highly respected pet authority, Michael Fox, D.Sc., Ph.D., B. Veterinary Medicine, M.R.C.V.S., in *Dr. Fox's Massage Program for Cats and Dogs,* writes, that touching a dog in the groin area is a friendly thing to do, the "equivalent of a human handshake." He adds that a dog presents his groin for contact to people and other dogs.

   The last people you'd expect to encourage one to touch a dog here are monks, but the monks of New Skete promulgate calming a dog down "by placing your open palm, over the dog's groin area...and hold [your hand] there." (The massage experts are the ones saying this so don't complain to us!)

   In *How to Be Your Dog's Best Friend* they also agree that this area is a traditional greeting place between fellow canines. "Dogs often tell each other 'it's all right' by nudging this area. When you gently place your hand there, it has the same effect on the dog as placing an arm around the shoulder..."

6. **In front of the tail:** Where your dog's tail ends and his pelvis begins is a sensitive, erogenous zone. By the way, many dogs reflexively raise their hind legs when rubbed here.

7. **Behind the ears**: Tickling or scratching a dog behind the ears may be sexual in its significance, because ear licking, sniffing, and nibbling are part of the preliminaries of canine courtship. In addition to scratching a dog behind the ears, some massage therapists will gently press the ears with the thumb and forefingers, although some dogs don't like that.

Touching the following three places almost always delights any dog, who will often immediately come back to you for more:

8. **Under the chin and the neck**: Stroke them without pressing or rubbing hard here, because you don't want to put any pressure on the windpipe or trachea.

9. **Behind the head at the base of the neck**: At the end of his neck, right before his spinal column begins, there are muscles that most dogs love to have gently massaged.

10. **Belly**: Rub it gently.

Most dogs like to have the following areas worked on:

11. **Between the ears**: Rub him lightly on the head between his ears. Puppies can practically become hypnotized when this is done to them.

12. **Temple area**: Do both sides at once.

13. **Top of the head**: Move the fur above the bone around gently by rotating it with your fingers and making little circles.

14. **Directly above the nose**: Very gently touching a dog here, in the area where there's no fur, sometimes just with the back of your hand, is also almost hypnotic for some dogs.

15. **The sides of the neck**: In some dogs you can do both sides at the same time by putting your hand around his neck and gently squeezing your fingers and thumb together.

16. **Along the muscles of the spine:** You can use both hands, but never rub too vigorously in the spinal region.

17. **Along the sides of the body**: Right down his ribs.

Some dogs love the following; for some it doesn't seem to do a thing; and others actively move away to avoid it:

18. **Both armpits (in the front legs)**: Don't touch here too forcefully. Many dogs like a light rubbing motion from inside the armpit down toward the body.

19. **Sides of the mouth**: Imagine a line continuing a few inches out from your dog's mouth and follow that line with one finger.

20. **Webbing in the back of the legs:** The webbing that connects the hind legs can be gently pressed with your thumb and forefinger. Don't do this for older dogs who may have arthritis and can be sensitive there. Incidentally, in *A Dog Is Listening,* Roger

Caras says that when dogs are playing, they sometimes nip each other in this area, confirming that it can be a sensitive and pleasurable area for many dogs.

21. **Between the toes**: Some dogs like being lightly pressed on the pads between the toes. Others are ticklish and move their feet away the minute you try to touch them there.

How to Do the Heimlich Maneuver
to Save Your Dog's Life

A man is choking; what do you do? The Heimlich maneuver. Your dog is choking; what do you do? Yes, you do the same thing but there is a major difference. When your dog is coming out of the trauma, confused, and dazed, he's more likely to bite you!

So be prepared, which shouldn't stop you from trying to save your dog's life with a modified Heimlich maneuver. We had it explained by Michelle Bamberger, D.V.M., of Massachusetts, who has taught emergency first aid for cats and dogs, and has written a book called *Help! The Quick Guide to First Aid for Your Dog.*

"It's not uncommon for a dog to choke because they swallow things they shouldn't, like small balls, toys, and bones," she says. "If an object becomes stuck, you'll see forceful coughing, possibly eyes bulging, and your dog will keep pawing at his mouth."

At this point you don't have much time. But even before you start the Heimlich maneuver, Dr. Bamberger says you should do the following:

- Open your dog's mouth to look for the object. Place one hand on the upper jaw with your thumb on one side and the rest of your fingers on the other side.

- With your other hand, push down on the lower jaw, keeping your index finger free to sweep back into the mouth.

- If you can see or feel the object, remove it.

- If there are two of you, one should hold your dog's mouth open, and the other look inside and remove the lodged object.

If you can't remove it that way, Dr. Bamberger advises you to try one more method of dislodging the object, since some say the

Does Shocking Dogs Really Hurt Them?

Many people think the use of electricity to help train dogs to stay in a fenced area, or to stop barking, is quite shocking. But Ross Becker, editor of *Good Dog!* magazine, tried one of these electric shock collars on himself several times, and reported that it wasn't all that bad. He also stressed that dogs have a lot of fur, and don't feel pain as strongly as we do.

But many people still believe that a person administering electric shock to a much smaller dog to change a natural behavior he or she finds offensive is just a howling shame.

Heimlich maneuver can break your dog's ribs and should not be your first choice.

- If your dog is small, hold him upside down, with his tail toward your face. Place your arms around his lower abdomen for thirty seconds while gently swaying him.

If that doesn't work, Dr. Bamberger gives you two versions of the Heimlich maneuver for dogs. Both are based on the "people" principle that thrusts on the diaphragm will dislodge the obstruction with compressed air.

- Place your dog on his side on a hard surface, tilted with his head down and his hindquarters up. If you can grab a pillow or rolled towel, put it under his hindquarters so the front of his body is lower than his back.

- With a small dog, place one hand on his back to steady him and the other under the center of the rib cage. Press in and up four to five times in a thrusting motion.

- With a large dog you'll need both hands for the thrust, so place both hands beneath the rib cage. Press in and up four to five times in a thrusting motion.

M.W. Harry, D.V.M., in his video "How to Save Your Dog's Life," outlines a Heimlich maneuver that does not call for laying your dog down. "Stand or kneel behind your dog. Grasp his body at the bottom of his rib cage. Apply firm quick pressure. Repeat two to five times."

Are Some Dogs Psychic?

Some swear that canine clairvoyance is a fact; others say it's all just a tall tale (tail?). But there are many hard-to-explain stories of dogs warning about impending disasters, of sensing dangers to themselves and their owners (even from a distance), of knowing things that would happen long before their owners did (including predicting the winners of the Triple Crown), or of allegedly rising (or "shining") as they died.

Disbelievers stress that these reports are anecdotal, self-deceptive or caused by cues unconsciously given by the owners. Nonetheless, many highly respected researchers and behaviorists are believers. For example, Dr. Michael Fox writes in *Superdog*: "Many animals, possibly your pet included, possess mental (or psychic) abilities far more sensitive and better developed than ours...[and are] far more aware of...another dimension of reality that is relatively closed to us."

Barbara Woodhouse makes no bones about a dog having "indisputable psychic powers—how else could a dog know when his owner's car, and his beloved owner, were approaching but still some miles away, or sense his owner's impending departure?...The evidence is overwhelming."

There actually are some dog psychics who, for forty to one hundred dollars an hour, will reveal a four-legged future. Some even tell of the past—a dog's past life, that is. One *Newsday* reporter decided to test the whole psychic question by going to an animal psychic for a "pet reading." This psychic, who charged reporter David Kocieniewski only three dollars, promised to reveal information about the reporter's dog's health, life span, whether he'll spawn offspring, and even his "career possibilities."

Although the psychic did say some things Kocieniewski felt she had no way of knowing, he also noted that the psychic said of his

Aromatherapy—and Crystals—for Dogs

A dog's sense of smell is far superior to that of humans, and since certain aromas have been proven beneficial to us, it makes sense (scents?) that aromatherapy would be applied to dogs as well.

In England, shopkeepers even sell special scents just for dogs, to be placed under their blankets, such as an essence of lavender and chamomile.

In Moab, Utah, Dr. Art Grusensky massages peppermint oil into a dog's skin to help rid the dog of intestinal gas, nausea, vomiting, and lethargy, according to *Dogs in Canada*.

At The Pet Department Store in New York City, which offers dog massages, they use a combination of sandalwood and jasmine.

And now, a Chicago company, Rosley's Rocks and Gems, has just put together ten pet *crystals* for dogs. The owner believes that amber is good for hyperactive dogs, and rose quartz is a "habit breaker."

"Why should only we humans benefit from the healing power of crystals? Why not share it with our four-legged…friends?" he asked in a *New Age* magazine article.

---

dog that "he likes people," just as the dog wagged his tail at a passer-by. Also, "'He's very affectionate,' she divined, as he rubbed his head on her leg," he wrote. The reporter was disappointed that the psychic couldn't help him "answer the Great Canine Mysteries: To neuter or not to neuter? Dry or canned? What's so tasty about dirty socks?"

Most animal psychics claim their abilities stem from mental images they receive from the dogs. But one may not have to be a professional to receive these. One California psychic offers a class for sixty dollars that teaches anyone how to understand and communicate telepathically with his or her pet.

In ancient times, almost everyone believed he or she could do that. Desmond Morris, in *Dogwatching*, writes that people even studied dogs' whines and growls, which were believed to warn of impending death and disaster. He says this belief may have arisen because dogs with rabies howled, whined, and made strange noises. If the dog infected its owner, who then died, this link between the dogs' cries and human death was interpreted as an omen by people before the transmission of infections was understood.

These days, many still don't know how some dogs seem to know when someone will die, or arrive home from some place when they're not expected. Disbelievers say the dogs are merely recognizing a particular style of walking, or a car motor before people can hear it. But there are many reports of dogs responding to events that happen in other cities.

It *is* known that dogs can appreciate the subtle differences and changes in the earth's electromagnetic field. Furthermore, they have four legs, not two, touching the ground. Then, too, not only do they have their extraordinarily keen senses of smell, but special detectors in their noses.

Older dog books often cite as proof of a canine's psychic ability the fact that Saint Bernards are able to tell whether a climber buried in an avalanche is alive by sniffing the snow. But researchers have now learned of sensitive heat detectors in dogs' noses which could enable them to detect body temperature through snow, and no more is written about "psychic Saint Bernards."

Perhaps, as we come to learn more about dogs and our environment, other "psychic" feats of dogs will one day also be explained in "logical" terms.

Or perhaps not.

The O.J. Simpson Case:
What the Akita Knows

The only known living witness to the Nicole Simpson murder is Kato—the dog, that is, not Kato Kaelin. But why didn't Kato (the dog) try to stop the murder, and why did he behave so oddly afterwards are questions that have had both dog experts and legal experts wondering.

We consulted three dog experts, including Akita specialist Barbara Bouyet, national coordinator of the Akita Rescue Society of America, and author of *Akita: Treasure of Japan.*

How do we know that Nicole's dog didn't try to ward off the attacker that night?

The dog wasn't blood splattered, nor did he have any knife marks on him. Considering the extensive wounds Ronald Goldman and Nicole Simpson sustained, the dog must have stayed away from the fray. "These are Japanese fighting dogs and very tenacious," says Bouyet of a breed once worshipped as gods and raised to protect the emperor in Japan. If the Akita had tried to protect his mistress, as one would expect, "The dog would have been knifed at the very least, and he probably would have been killed trying to defend her."

Why didn't the Akita attack the killer that night?

Bouyet believes the dog not only knew the killer—but it was probably a boss to the dog. "An Akita will attack someone harming his family—unless it's another dominant household member. O.J. Simpson would have been the alpha [pack leader] male to the dog, and Nicole the alpha female. And Akitas don't interfere with alpha males and alpha females."

Is there a precedence for such behavior by a dog?

A few years ago movie actress Susan Cabot was murdered by

Dogs Can Improve Your Marriage

An Indiana University study of thirty married couples showed that husbands and wives were better able to resolve their marital conflicts when their dog was in the room.

When the dogs were present, the couples were less tense and angry, and able to work out their differences better, according to this study, reported in the *National Enquirer*. In addition, their heart rates and blood pressures were lower, a finding in keeping with other studies.

Psychologist Elayne Kahn believes that dogs not only calm couples but strengthen marriages in general. "I think almost as many marriages stay together because of the dog as because of the children," joked the Miami psychologist. "A dog provides continuity and conversation for the couple, and something to care for and love together. The dog is a continuing source of pleasure that gives husbands and wives something to talk about with each other and with others."

Dr. Kahn believes that having a dog is better for many marriages than having children—and that the dog may bring the couples more pleasure. "Unlike children, dogs don't go through an adolescent or adult rebellion. They more openly show their love than children do. And while the children may not have turned out the way the couple hoped, their dog probably did.

---

her son, and her two Akitas didn't protect her. "Why?" asks Bouyet. "Because the fight was between an alpha male and an alpha female." (By the way, the two dogs ended up in a shelter; one died there, and Bouyet took in the other.)

Did Nicole's Akita do anything strange after the murder?

People reported that they heard strange howls of a confused and anguished dog. "These are quiet dogs," she says. "They hunt silently like cats. The kind of noise that was described as coming from an Akita made my blood curdle; it was an Akita absolutely torn to pieces. He did not understand why this whole thing was happening, and I think he was confused because the person attacking his mistress was not an outsider."

Did the dog try to help Nicole in any way?

"There was blood on the dog's underbelly, so, I think he must have lain over his dying or dead mistress after the killer left," says Bouyet. "That's typical of the loyalty of an Akita."

What did the dog do when he saw O.J. Simpson later that was so unusual?

When O.J. arrived back home in his white Bronco, the Akita, who had been taken to O.J.'s home, was sitting in the middle of the island. "When they showed it on the Channel 7 news, everyone was watching the Bronco, but I was watching the dog. And that dog did not act normal. He did not greet O.J. He did not go up to anyone in the car, which is abnormal for an Akita. They're very responsive when you return home, and greet you enthusiastically.

"But that dog looked into the car, *stiffened, backed up, barked, and backed up again* when he saw O.J.," she remembers. Why did the dog show such defensive behavior? "I don't believe that an Akita would ever behave that way toward someone unless that person had done something bad," she says. And *Newsday* included in a November 13, 1994, essay that Akita experts believe, "From the depths of his loyal, ruined heart, Kato [was saying to O.J.] 'You. You. It was you.'"

A highly respected pathologist, Dr. Cyril Wecht, said that if the dog was brought into court, he might be able to identify the killer. Do dog experts agree?

Bouyet believes that if the trial had taken place immediately after the murder, and if the dog had again "backed up and barked, or cowered or showed submission when he saw O.J.," that would be telling.

Wes Patterson, owner of Good Shepherd Dog Training, concurs. He said on CNN that if the killer and the dog were put together right after the murder, the dog "will immediately go to avoidance and want to stay away from that person."

But things might be different later. "Dogs are not going to develop something like that weeks or months afterwards," says famous dog trainer, actor, and author Arthur J. (Captain) Haggerty. "The dog wouldn't look at someone and say, 'Oh, you're the guy who killed my mistress and now I'm going to get you. I didn't do it before because I was too busy.' They're not elephants.

"People carry grudges because they dwell on it and then it becomes worse," he adds. "A dog is not going to think about something and say, 'That son of a bitch did this or that to me.' Two weeks later they're not going to remember the incident.

"To get a dog to carry a grudge, you have to do something really super violent from the dog's point of view, like some great bodily harm to them. But even if someone tried to kill the dog, he wouldn't realize the concept."

Anything else about this dog?

Yes. Sherry Carpenter, Pennsylvania author and educator, relates some interesting facts about the Akita:

- The first person to import the Akita into the United States was Helen Keller.

- The Akita is a fine swimmer and an excellent water dog. One of O.J.'s children by his first wife died of drowning. Could this dog have been chosen—consciously—with the thought that he might one day be able to save someone in trouble?

- If so, not only did he not live up to expectations, but she adds that "this breed is considered a symbol of good health and good fortune in Japan."

- All the attention on the Akita in the O.J. Simpson case may make them overly popular. "That type of notoriety victimizes a breed," she laments, "so dogs may end up in shelters when one hundred and ten pounds becomes too much to feed and walk and groom."

How to Get Your Dog on David Letterman's Stupid Pet Tricks

Your dog will have a better chance of getting on David Letterman's Stupid Pet Tricks if the trick looks good in slow-motion instant replay—like the dog who can catch a Frisbee blindfolded—or there's something unusual about it, like it plays well backward as well as forward.

That doesn't mean the dog has to know it or do it backwards. In one of their funniest segments, the trick was slow-action *videoed* backward as well as forward. "We had a Lab once who caught spewed ice cream that the owner would spit out of his mouth. It was hilarious in slow motion when the dog would catch it—but it was even funnier when we played it *backward*, in slow motion, and the dog appeared to be tossing the ice cream back into the owner's mouth," recalls Susan Hall Sheehan, the segment producer.

Even if the not-so-stupid trick your dog does can only be played forward, he might still make it on the show. "The tricks don't have to be spectacular. Some are fun and silly," she says, recalling her eleven years of producing this segment. "What we're looking for has evolved over the years," she explains. "We're always looking to go one step beyond what we've done. For example, at one point we would have just wanted a dog sitting up on its hind legs. But then it became a dog balancing a biscuit on its nose while sitting up on its hind legs, to a dog flipping the biscuit off his nose while sitting up on his hind legs, to a dog flipping a biscuit off his nose while sitting up on his hind legs *while blindfolded*," she laughs.

Singing dogs, unless there's something extra to it, generally don't make it. "We've done a lot of singing dogs, like the spaniel who sang the nightly news theme. Now, we're looking for something beyond that. For example, we just had a singing family of Airedales, a mother and two daughters, that only sang to 'Happy Birthday.'

Publications That May Print Photos of Your Dog

1. *Workman's 365 Dogs Page-A-Day Color Calendar* uses contest-winning photos. Entry forms are on the front page of each calendar, or write Workman Publishing, Grand Central Station, P.O. Box 3927, New York, N.Y. 10163. The deadline is February 1, but the contest is annual.

2. *Dogs USA*. You may submit up to three entries in each category: happy dogs or two or more dogs. Prizes include publication and up to $150. The deadline is May 15, but the contest is annual. Get entry form from: Dogs USA, P.O. Box 6050, Mission Viejo, CA 92690.

3. *Dog Fancy* prints four to six photos per issue in their "Gallery." Include your dog's name, breed or mix along with your own name, address, city, state, and phone number. Send to: Dog Fancy Gallery, P.O. Box 6050, Mission Viejo, CA 92690.

4. *Mighty Dog Calendar,* sponsored by the Friskies PetCare Company, has twelve winners, mostly in theme photos. Send thirty UPC symbols from cans of Mighty Dog dog food, or $5.99 with no proof of purchase. The deadline is April 1, but the contest is annual. Mighty Dog Calendar Offer, P.O. Box 1151, Young America, MN 55594.

5. *Globe's* Pet Photo is a weekly contest. $75 award. Send to: Globe Pet Photo, 5401 N.W. Broken Sound Blvd., Boca Raton, FL 33487.

6. *National Enquirer's Reader's* Photo of the Week is often of a dog. Prize is $50, plus a chance to win their $1,000 Photo of the Year award. Rules are in the newspaper, and photos should be sent to "Photo of the Week," National Enquirer, Lantana, FL 33464.

NOTE: most places don't return or acknowledge photos.

Your dog doesn't have to sing to be turned down by this show. "We get a lot of Boston terriers who love balloons," says Ms. Sheehan, who owns a Boston terrier herself. "I don't know what it is about that little flat face but they love to go after balloons. Dalma-

277 Secrets Your Dog Wants You to Know

tians and other breeds are big on bubbles. Rottweilers and bulldogs like skateboards, while dachshunds like tennis or pool balls. I've seen some dachshunds who chase billiard balls down into the pockets of pool tables."

Dogs playing dead, speaking, counting, understanding other languages, or playing soccer are routinely refused. Furthermore, pet tricks considered stupid enough for the show are not taught in obedience classes. "We don't want dogs who have been taught to crawl, or zigzag between their owner's legs. That's an ability, not a trick. We're looking for *tricks* that are on the edge of reality."

One problem is that even if your dog does the trick at home, he may not do it at a studio, *and* on command. "One dog could tuck his three legs together underneath him like he was on his elbows, and then do a pirouette. It was hysterical," she chuckles.

"But when he got here, he had no clue as to what it was that he was supposed to do. He was friendly and he wanted to play. Some dogs want to run around and sniff the band equipment, or say hello to the camera man. There's so much else going on here that doing their trick may be the farthest thing from their minds. If it's a trick the dog loves to do, you'll have a better chance getting him past the distractions."

To protect themselves, generally six dogs are brought in for the segment, and only three actually appear on the show. That may cause the owner to lose heart, or face, but never any money. The owners of all dogs chosen for the segment receive travel expenses, plus one hundred dollars or so additional to cover incidentals for the day, which is spent rehearsing.

Tricks that make it must also be safe for the dogs who voluntarily perform them. That means no putting out cigarettes, or dogs that are manipulated to look like people or creatures. Nor should they be spun on the floor for break dancing. "When break dancing came out, I got a million of those."

If you think your pet qualifies, call 212-975-5952 and leave a description of what he can do on Ms. Sheehan's voice mail. She'll call you back if she's interested, so you won't have to go through all the hassle of making a tape to find out they've already had another dog do the trick on the show.

If she is interested, she will ask you to send a tape to The Late Show, 1697 Broadway, New York, NY 10019, attention "Stupid Pet Tricks" Department. But if the trick is truly astounding, she says to go ahead and send in the tape without the advance call.

They like videotapes in this department, which receives about 150 mail and video applications each week. "It's helpful now that people have accessibility to video cameras, because instead of having to hold live auditions and being limited to people in the tri-state area, people can send in videotapes and show the trick being done. But have your dog do it a few times in a row without stopping, or editing, so we can see that the animal is consistent," she says.

And if he can do it backward, all the better.

Do Dogs Go to Heaven?

Animals and man have been closely allied spiritually for years. Indeed, many types of animals, not just dogs, have been recognized religiously. In 1987, an Italian nun claimed God spoke to her through her parakeet, and in 1989, at the Feast of St. Francis in New York, a bowl of algae was consecrated, according to the *First Pet History of the World*.

Our main interest here is dogs, however, so we spoke with five theologians who espouse different religions, and asked them what they believed about this issue:

> *Christians generally believe that people go to heaven through their belief in Jesus Christ, and since dogs don't believe in Him, they would not. But many Christians like myself do not exclude others from life after death, and we believe there are many different paths to God.*
>
> *I'm a Methodist minister, and our founder, John Wesley, rode his horse everywhere, preaching. He firmly believed his horse went to heaven because he loved his horse, which served him faithfully. So, from his point of view, it is possible that he would have made that extension, that dogs would also go to heaven. I don't see why not.*
>
> —REVEREND JULIE PARKER, protestant chaplain at
> Hofstra University in Hempstead, New York

> *We think of heaven as like looking at a puzzle with some of the pieces missing. We can't solve that puzzle because we can't know what happens until we die and by then we can't call home.*
>
> *Nobody knows for sure if animals are in heaven because nobody knows for sure if animals have souls. They definitely don't have souls exactly like our souls because they can't decide between good and bad.*

How Your Dog Can Be a Hero

Many people have bad things to say about pit bulls, but during the California floods of 1993, one saved the lives of thirty people, twenty-nine dogs, thirteen horses, and one cat. He did this by carrying food to the stranded animals and people, and leading them to less turbulent areas where they could safely cross over.

He was a hero, like the shepherd a few years earlier who entered a snake pit to pull out a child, and other dogs who fought off attacks by wild animals, prevented drownings, burglaries, or death by fire. And all became winners of the Ken-L Ration Dog Hero of the Year Award.

According to the director of professional services for the Pet Food Division of Ken-L Ration, Steve Willett, three hundred to four hundred animals each year are entered by their owners (or stories about them are clipped from newspapers) for this contest. The winner receives a year's supply of Kibbles 'n Bits dog food, and his owner get a silver-plated dog bowl. That's all? No money? Well, the dog is the one who deserves everything and he can't spend money anyway.

So go ahead and nominate your dog for the glory (and the dog food), if you think he qualifies. For guidelines, send a self-addressed stamped envelope to Ken-L Ration Dog Hero of the Year Award, P.O. Box 1370, Barrington, IL 60011.

Even though their souls are different, is God's love for animals big enough to bring them to heaven? We believe that God also loves animals enough to do this wonderful thing for them. So when you die, you may see your dog again—and also your goldfish who you flushed down your toilet—so be careful!

—MONSIGNOR THOMAS HARTMAN, director of radio and
television for the Diocesan Television Center in
Uniondale, New York, and coauthor with
Rabbi Marc Gellman of *Where Does God Live?*

Most of Judaism focuses on how we act in this world, and there's not too much speculation on what goes on in the next world. We don't know exactly who goes to heaven or why, and since we don't know, maybe dogs do go to heaven.

277 Secrets Your Dog Wants You to Know

Within Judaism, one must be kind to animals because we will then develop ourselves as kinder and gentler and more compassionate human beings, and ultimately treat other human beings with more gentleness and kindness. And we hope that on the basis of treating people kindly, we will go to heaven, or to the world to come, or wherever we go when we die.

—RABBI NEIL COOPER, Temple Beth Hillel-Beth El, Wynnewood, Pennsylvania

Dogs don't have souls so far as we know; I therefore have no mandate for saying whether they will or will not go to heaven. But I have to trust God's kindness that there's something I don't know that makes provision for that.

The love dogs give to humans somehow cannot be lost into nothingness. The fact that He created such a beautiful thing as a dog is very obviously part of His pattern and plan for our joy and the joy of humanity.

—FATHER JOHN ANDREW, former chaplain to the Archbishop of Canterbury and rector of St. Thomas Church, an Anglican church in Manhattan

We are taught that heaven is for human beings, and that when animals die, whether they are cats or dogs, they turn back into dust the way they were before, and that is the end of the animals.

But the way people treat animals may determine whether they go to heaven or hell. Islam teaches people to be compassionate to all creatures of God, animals and humans, and to take care of each other. Prophet Mohammed said that a sinner who shared water with a thirsty dog, bringing it up from a well in her shoe, went to heaven when she died because of her compassionate act.

But a person who tied their cat up in their house, preventing him from getting food and water so the cat died, went to hell because they prevented the animal from finding its own way to survive.

—AL-HAAJ GHAZI KHANKAN, director of interfaith and communications at the Islamic Center of Long Island, Westbury, New York

We also asked a theology scholar, Scott S. Smith, author of *Pet Souls: Evidence That Animals Survive Death*, to summarize some of the other religious positions:

> *Buddhism doesn't say that dogs go to heaven, because they don't believe anything survives death except Karma. They're vague about what happens when you achieve nirvana.*
>
> *The Hindus are of two minds on the subject, but in neither one do you have dogs going to heaven. In one form, there is no reality. We don't last, nothing is permanent, and there are no individual souls. So dogs do not go to heaven because there's no such things as dogs or human beings.*
>
> *In another branch of Hinduism, they believe in souls, but they don't go to heaven either. They just get reincarnated in different forms, so your dog may end up as your cat.*
>
> *Shinto: They believe everything has a soul: rocks, water, and, yes, dogs. They will all go to heaven.*

In conclusion, Smith says that "Here there are more animals than people in this world and most religions don't even have anything definite to say about it. Isn't it incredible?"

A few other quotes are also worth including:

> *A few years ago I conducted a survey of British veterinarians.... One out of five...believed that a dog has a soul and an afterlife.... When the same survey was applied a year later to practicing veterinarians in Japan, every single veterinarian surveyed believed that dogs have souls and an afterlife.*
>
> —BRUCE FOGLE, *A Dog's Mind*

> *You think dogs will not be in heaven? I tell you, they will be there long before any of us.*
>
> —ROBERT LOUIS STEVENSON

> *If we have souls, then dogs have souls, and if we go to heaven, so do they.... Because if dogs are not there...it is not heaven.*
>
> —ELIZABETH MARSHALL THOMAS, author of
> *The Secret Life of Dogs,* in *Newsweek*

90 Little-Known Dangers
That Could Harm Your Dog

Sadly, most people don't know about the common hazards that face—and often kill—dogs daily. The media only occasionally publicizes these stories, focusing solely on bizarre local cases, like the cocker spaniel who baked to death under an automatic hair dryer when the attendant forgot about him.

The dog who died after eating a tampon also got some coverage, but only because the Illinois government official who owned him actually appointed a special prosecutor to investigate the incident. (The veterinarian who treated the dog had his license suspended for forty-five days.)

If more attention were focused on the day-to-day hazards that dogs face, a lot of canine lives could be saved. Occasionally someone writes a letter to a dog magazine, warning others of some danger. But most dog owners are painfully unaware of all the pitfalls their pets regularly face.

Even if you don't read the following story in its entirety, at least glance down at the bolded words so you will be aware of some potential perils for your pet, and can take measures to protect your dog.

Indoor Hazards

Kitchen: Not only are some **bones** dangerous, but so is the **twine** used to truss the food, or any string, because these can get caught in the dog's intestines and cause a blockage if swallowed. Watch out also for glass or plastic **thermometers,** which the dog may eat if he gulps down the rest of the bird when you're not looking.

Pot and **pan handles** should always be turned inward to avoid bumping them and spilling **boiling liquids** on the dog. Be careful with **oven cleaners,** which are poisonous.

Bathroom: Because of a dog's smaller size and slower metabolism, some medicines cause a more intensified reaction than they would in humans. Don't give dogs **diet pills, heart pills,** or **sleeping pills**. Don't give him two **aspirin** and figure you'll call the vet in the morning. Don't give him **acetaminophen, Tylenol, Datril, Advil, Motrin,** or **Ibuprofen**—in fact, don't give him any human medicine without consulting with your veterinarian first.

Also: **feminine hygiene products, pantyhose or stockings,** and **diapers** can be attractive to dogs, but can cause blockages, etc. **Toilet-bowl cleaners** are caustic so keep the toilet lid down. Keep **disposable twin razor blades, hair peroxides, nail polish remover, deodorants, deodorizers, disinfectants, drain cleaner, dye, laxatives, nail polish, permanent wave lotion, rubbing alcohol, soaps, cleaning fluids,** and **asthma inhalers** out of your dog's reach.

All around the house: **Bleach** is bad. So is **boric acid**, which people put down for roaches. Watch out for **mothballs, kerosene, fungicides, furniture polish, matches, lye, metal polish, mineral spirits, phenol, photographic developer, shoe polish, tar,** and **window washing solution**. Also **lead** (which can also be found in **linoleum, paint, batteries, foil, golf balls,** and many other items). **Pennies** minted since 1982 contain 96 percent zinc, which can cause zinc poisoning. Also **turpentine** and construction items like **glue, wood preservatives,** and so forth.

There have been anecdotal reports of puppies or small dogs being killed when they jumped up from under glass **cocktail tables** in the living room, or down from a high **dining table** that they climbed on to get food. Dogs with damp paws have skidded on wet tile right **through glass doors** and **windows**, even through supposedly shatterproof glass. It may happen when they're chasing bugs, butterflies, or whatever. There are also stories of animals **licking newly polished floors,** so keep dogs out of the room until the floor dries.

Sewing thread and **needles** are particularly appetizing to dogs, but they, too, can cause intestinal blockage if swallowed. **Lamp cords** can be dangerous to both of you. If a live wire is still in his mouth, disconnect the cord so you don't get a shock as well.

Flea Products, Collars, and Muzzles

Problems with flea control products are a common source of calls to poison control centers. For example, **flea dips** may harm your dog if he has a skin problem with open sores. Always follow the instructions carefully; for example, brush the excess flea powder off your dog thirty minutes after it is applied. The product labels often provide a toll-free number for information concerning usage if you're confused.

Any **collar** can cause problems or death. A cocker spaniel puppy in Florida had a simple snap collar that got caught in a portable kennel and he was killed. A dog may pull on a **choke chain**, and suddenly halt, causing spinal injuries. The ASPCA warns not to tie animals outside wearing a choke collar at all, or they can literally choke. Use a buckle collar instead, even those too can present dangers. A dog in Texas got the ring around his collar caught on rose bushes.

Elizabethan collars, those cone-shaped oversized collars dogs sometimes have to wear on their heads for medical reasons, may be necessary, but be more watchful than usual if your dog is wearing one. There are at least two reported cases of dogs in these collars putting their heads into plastic bags, like those inside cereal boxes, and then being unable to paw the plastic off. Also watch your dog if he's wearing a **muzzle**. If he vomits, with his mouth closed, he can't spit anything out, and some dogs have choked to death.

Cars

Letting dogs ride in the rear bed of a **pickup truck covered by tarpaulin** or a rigid plastic cap can cause death from **carbon monoxide poisoning**. (That can also kill dogs indoors, just as it can a person, as in the case of Vitas Gerulaitis.)

Leaving the back uncovered may be even more dangerous. **Loose dogs in the back of an open truck** can easily be knocked out if you hit an unexpected pothole or slam on the brakes suddenly. Or they may **jump out** to chase a passing cat, dog, or squirrel. They can also **strangle** to death if they are leashed and jump.

They can **burn the pads of their paws** because the **bed of a truck** can get as hot as the rest of the car in the summer months.

Riding there, or in the back of an open car, or with their heads sticking out of a car window, also makes them—especially their eyes—vulnerable to injury from **flying foreign objects**. For example, a dog in New Orleans died when a tree branch hit him as the truck was going 60 miles per hour.

There are also dangers when dogs are left **inside the car.** Left alone in a parked car in the summer heat, they can bake. In the winter, the car can turn into a refrigerator.

While a car is moving, dogs in the front seat can hit the dashboard and be crushed from a sudden stop. Or if they crawl under the **back window**, they could turn into a flying missile if the car stops abruptly.

And don't ever put your **dog in the trunk**. It would seem obvious, but the *New Orleans Times-Picayune* reported that many people who drive up to the LASPCA, open the trunk and pull out one or more animals. Incredibly, one woman said she did it because she didn't want to dirty the inside of her nice car!

Even if the car is just in the garage, and your dog isn't in it, there are dangers. If your dog drinks **brake fluid**, **carburetor cleaner**, or **gasoline**, it's potentially lethal. **Antifreeze** (ethylene glycol) causes thousands of dog deaths each year. It can collect in a puddle under a parked car, attracting your dog with its sweet aroma. By the time symptoms appear (which may include loss of appetite, unquenchable thirst and a stumbling gait), it may be too late. Go to your veterinarian immediately if you suspect your dog has consumed one of these fluids.

Outdoors

Water-related: Even clean-looking water can be contaminated by animals or chemicals. When traveling, carry bottled water for both of you. Watch where your dog drinks. That means no lakes, rivers, or puddles. Other water dangers can come from **blue-green algae**, or **ocean water**, which can make dogs seriously ill if they drink too much of it. **Pool chemicals**, especially undiluted chlorine, are another water-related menace.

Dogs have died when they tried to walk across a **frozen pond** or **stream**. Their owners have also died trying to save them.

Lawn-related: Some dogs eat weird nonfood items (called pica), including **rocks.** Other eat **grass**, which may have been treated with chemicals such as **fertilizer** or **weed killer.** Read the labels carefully, and keep the products out of reach. Use your sprinkler or hose to help the chemicals sink in, unless the directions state otherwise. Keep your dogs off the lawn for twenty-four hours afterward, or until it is dry, whichever comes first.

Watch out for **insecticides, herbicides**, or **other chemicals** applied to your lawn, shrubbery, or trees. A lot has been written lately about an herbicide, **2,4-D**, used in fifteen hundred different weed killing products, which has been linked to malignant lymphoma in dogs.

Miscellaneous outdoors: Curbing a dog at a **bus stop** is risky; the driver is so high up he sometimes doesn't see the dog. **Rotting garbage** puts your dog at risk because it smells great to him. Secure your outdoor garbage with tight lids. (Indoors, **rotten food** that dogs have jumped up and stolen off a table or counter has caused more deaths than people realize.)

The Tragedy of the Dog and the Diaper

The unexpected and unnecessary death of any dog is a horror, but an especially sad case occurred in Pennsylvania in March of 1993. Many dogs are naturally attracted to soiled diapers, as was one basset hound who accidentally ingested a small amount of a disposable baby diaper.

The dog vomited up some of it, but the rest remained in his body, spewing out toxins. He lingered for three and a half months before dying.

The owner wrote to *Dog World* that when she contacted the diaper manufacturer to inform them of what happened, they sent her a leaflet and some coupons so she could purchase more diapers from them.

What we use to kill rats may be more dangerous than the rats, because **rodent killer** (which may also be used indoors) can be a dog killer as well. (Symptoms can start two to five days after ingestion and much of the bleeding can be internal, so you might not realize what's happened.)

Dogs can be injured by **poisonous insects** (especially one called striped walking stick), **spiders, snakes**, and so forth. (Look for swellings on the body.) Also, **products used to kill other animals and insects**, especially those for controlling garden snails and slugs, can kill your dog. Secondary poisonings are also a possibility; birds and others eat the poisoned items, become ill or die, and they in turn may be eaten by dogs and cats.

Outdoors, **fishhooks** can become embedded in a dog's body, especially if a fisherman leaves old bait on his line, which can attract a dog. Other outdoor nonfatal but painful hazards include **foxtails, cacti, thistles**, and **sand spurs**.

Wild animals present **rabies** problems, especially **raccoons** (be wary of lethargic or friendly acting ones), **skunks, opossums, woodchucks, rabbits,** and **bats**. And **porcupine quills** can end up in your dog's nose or mouth and be excruciatingly painful.

Still awake? Believe it or not, there are many more hazards. The important thing is to be cautious and watchful, and if your dog has sudden unexplained signs of illness like vomiting, diarrhea, or seizures, to call your vet immediately.

Or call the University of Illinois National Animal Poison Control Center, at (800) 548-2423. It costs $30 (major credit cards accepted) for as many calls as the case requires.

For quick questions, or if you don't have a credit card, call their other number, (900) 680-0000. It costs $20 for the first five minutes and $2.95 for each additional minute.

These 19 Products Could
Save Your Dog's Life

1. **If someone in your family is allergic to your dog,** there's no need to consider getting rid of your pet. Rub Allerpet on your dog and most allergy problems disappear.

    Available in many pet stores and catalogue houses, like Pet Warehouse, in Xenia, Ohio.

2. **If your dog is too old to get up and down** there is PawsWay, a ramp for older dogs, or any dog with limited mobility, who can't jump up and down from the bed, couch, or any favorite spot because of arthritis, age, injury, postoperative healing, or back problems. Available from Pet Care with Love, Inc.

3. **What if you were hit by a car while your dog was home?** Have you ever considered what would happen to your dog if you were in a fatal accident, or with memory loss somewhere? Would someone know that your dog was home waiting for you? A Pet Alert Wallet Card warns people that you've got a dog back home who needs to be cared for. Someone will find this and hopefully see that your dog is cared for.

4. **What if there's a fire? Will anyone know your dog is in the house?** The Pet Alert kit includes an inside doorknob safety information hanger; a plastic doorknob bag to enclose photographs; and reflective Pet Alert stickers to be placed outside the front entrance and/or window. Available from Pet Alert.

5. **You need a leash with lights if you walk your dog at night.** The Light Up Dog Leash is a four-foot lead with light elements every four inches, and a plastic handle with an on/off switch. Includes 9-volt battery. Available from Doctors Foster & Smith.

277 Secrets Your Dog Wants You to Know

6. **If your dog won't let you brush his teeth**, slip these Finger Brushes, or tooth brushes, over your fingers. Brushing your dog's teeth can protect him from tooth decay and tartar buildup that could shorten his life. Package includes two brushes: one for gum massage; one for toothbrushing. This product is available from many catalogues and stores including Pedigrees, in Bradenton, Florida.

7. **If your dog still won't let you brush his teeth, how about a poultry-flavored toothpaste?** With fluoride, no less. If your dog hates to have his teeth brushed, even with the finger brushes above, get right to the root of the problem by buying something he'll like. The best part is that this paste doesn't have to be rinsed out afterward, so you only have to go into your dog's mouth once. Available from Cherrybrook, in Broadway, New Jersey.

8. **Do you use sunscreen on your dog?** Most people don't, but look at the chapter "Dogs Need Sunscreen, Too!" (page 141) and you'll soon change your mind. "Sun Spot" claims to be "the only sun protection product specifically designed for pets." It's PABA free, provides UVA and UVB protection, and contains emollients to protect your dog against dryness, too. It also contains oil of citronella, a natural insect repellent—so it might scare away the bugs of summer as well. Available from Pet Warehouse, in Xenia, Ohio.

9. **At last! A double-loop leash for dogs who are hard to walk.** Owners of large dogs will appreciate GRRRIP, a two-handled dog leash with the second looped handle near the collar. This keeps you from hurting your wrist by having to wrap the leash around your hand, and also keeps your dog from getting away. It comes in four- and six-foot lengths. Available from Crowd Pleaser Pet Products.

10. **If you want to protect your dog's eyes from the sun,** sunglasses will do the trick—while making him look like a movie star. They can also save his life by preventing blindness, which is often a reason older dogs are put to sleep. Customized UV-protective sunglasses that stay on most dogs are available. Send breed name and weight to Allen/Carter.

The 5 Best Dog Books for Children

We asked the owners of New York City's Dog Lovers Bookshop, Bern Marcowitz and Margot Rosenberg, for their opinions on the best dog books for children, since they have a large selection of childrens' books at the store, and both of them have a literary background. Here's the list they came up with:

How Dogs Really Work!, by Alan Snow (Little, Brown and Company, ages 4 to 8).

Lassie Come Home, by Eric Knight, illustrated by Marguerite Kirmse (Henry Holt, ages 8 and up).

Moe the Dog in Tropical Paradise, by Diane Stanley (Putnam, ages 4 to 8).

Only One Woof, by James Herriot, illustrated by Peter Barrett (St. Martin's Press, ages 6 to 9).

Ten Little Puppy Dogs, by Lisa McCue (Random House, preschool).

All of these books may be available in your local library, your child's school, or at a local bookstore. They may also be ordered from the Dog Lovers Bookshop, 9 West 31st St., New York, NY 10001, (212) 594-3601.

11. **What if your dog's collar accidentally catches on something?** This Dog Safety Collar automatically releases to prevent strangulation if the collar accidentally catches on a fence, branch, or whatever. Adjustable, one-inch double nylon webbing. Available in several colors, including neon. Available from SavYor Pet Products.

12. **Just finding the tick isn't enough**; you have to be able to remove it without squeezing its body. Pro-Tick Remedy safely removes ticks, and fits on your key chain. The twenty-four karat gold-plated instrument comes with tick capture bags and antiseptic pads. Available from Safety Consulting Services, Ltd.

13. **You're not the only one who needs to wear a life vest on a boat.** Aqua-Pet is a bright orange-yellow life vest that comes

with reflective strips, foam for extra warmth and cushioning, D-ring for tethering, and a handle to help you grab your dog. You can even have your dog's name embroidered on one side, and the name of your boat on the other. Available from Windborne Products.

14. **A paralyzed dog does not have to be put to sleep.** Dogs with paralyzed rear legs, or injured or aging dogs, can now get around with a K-9 cart, which attaches to their back legs. Available from K-9 Carts.

15. **A dog in the front seat could be a flying missile if your car stops suddenly.** This Car Safety Strap for Pets is a seat belt that snaps into your car's existing seat belt buckle, while the other end attaches to your pet's harness or collar. Adjustable. Blue only. Call first to check if it will fit your vehicle. Available from Discount Master Animal Care.

16. **Your dog needs a passport as much as you.** If you're traveling with your dog, Sam's Dog Passport has sections for owner and pet information, and a place for a photo. If you're staying home, use it to keep track of vaccinations and medical treatments. Available from Sam's Pet Passports.

Audio- and Videotapes

17. **If your dog is afraid of thunder or fireworks,** try this audio tape and training program that includes the sounds of thunder, fireworks, gun shots, sirens, babies crying, crowd noise, lawn equipment, and more. Available from K-9 Counterconditioning.

18. **Teach your dog to be a Canine Good Citizen.** When a dog doesn't fit into the family, he may be taken to a shelter; teaching your dog to be a Good Citizen also strengthens the human-animal bond. This videotape teaches you how to inspect your dog's appearance and grooming, and how to help him react to other dogs and strangers. Available from The Latham Foundation.

19. **Children are most often the victims of dog bites.** This videotape program for children teaches them how to keep from

Experimenting on Dogs by Students

Between five and six million animals in America—including dogs—are used in experiments each year, some by junior high and high school students, says the ASPCA. Chillingly, there is no law limiting what a researcher may do to an animal as part of an experiment.

The ASPCA writes that high school students "may be encouraged to do animal-based science projects...often involv[ing] administration of painful stimuli or noxious substances, or even surgery of animals.... Unlike biomedical research experiments, whose purpose is to gather new data, most educational projects are nothing more than repetitive exercises...performed by students who are untrained in surgical techniques...caus[ing] pain and stress to countless animals, yet provid[ing] no new or useful information."

They advocate developing more alternatives like the Resusci-dog, a model dog used to teach students to perform CPR, which makes the use of a real dog unnecessary.

being bitten by a dog. "Safety Is Fun" includes a fifteen-minute tape, coloring poster, and lesson plan for teachers. Available from Glencoe Animal Hospital.

NOTE: In this chapter, in others on unusual items and expensive ones, and elsewhere throughout this book, we mention a number of products. This does not imply an endorsement for them nor are we responsible for what happens if you purchase them. We have not been paid to mention them. We tried out very few of them, and paid for those we did. We included them not because we are recommending them but rather as a point of interest.

In addition, some mail-order companies go out of business quickly and catalogue houses may stop stocking items, so some things we mention may no longer be available. You may also find some of the items at the larger chain pet department stores, such as Petco, Petsmart, or Petstuff.

Ordering Information:

1. Pet Warehouse. (800) 443-1160. 12 oz. $5.75 + $4.75 s/h.

2. Pet Care with Love, Inc., P.O. Box 764, Glenview, IL 60025. (800) 441-1765. $65-$130.

3. Animal-Vues, RD #2, Box 71, Bloomsburg, PA 17815. $2, plus SASE.

4. Pet Alert, P.O. Box 1690-B, Garden Grove, CA 92642. $8.95 ea.+ $1.50 s/h.

5. Doctors Foster & Smith. (800) 826-7206. $9.98 + s/h.

6. Pedigrees. (800) 548-4786. $8.99 + $4.99 s/h.

7. Cherrybrook. (800) 524-0820. Petrodex, 6 oz. for $3.85 + $2.75 s/h.

8. Pet Warehouse. (800) 443-1160. $9.79 + $4.75 s/h.

9. Crowd Pleaser Pet Products, 8A Village Loop, Ste. 196, Pomona, CA 91766. $12.

10. Allen/Carter, P.O. Box 1112, Osprey, FL 34229. $7 + $1.50 s/h.

11. SavYor Pet Products, P.O. Box 352, Lafayette Hill, PA 19444. $8.95

12. Safety Consulting Services, Ltd., P.O. Box 573, 8 Bulsontown Rd., Stony Point, NY 10980. $7.

13. Windborne Products, 201 Cypress Pl., Sausalito, CA 94965, (415) 331-5115. $45-85.

14. K-9 Carts, P.O. Box 160639, Big Sky, MT 59716, (800) 578-6960. $190-$335 + $16 s/h.

15. Discount Master Animal Care. (800) 346-0749. $11.99 +5.95 s/h.

16. Sam's Pet Passports, 22320 Bryant St., West Hills, CA 91304. $2.50.

17. K-9 Counter Conditioning, 1321 Longmeadow Dr., Glenview, IL 60025. $19.95 + $3 s/h.

18. The Latham Foundation, Latham Plaza Bldg., Clement & Schiller Streets, Alameda, CA 94501. $35.

19. Glencoe Animal Hospital, 3712 N. High St., Columbus, OH 43214. $49.95.

How to Teach Your Dog
to Sing–and Then
How to Shut Him Up

Teaching dogs to sing isn't that difficult. What's hard is getting them to sing when *you* like, rather than when *they* want—such as three o'clock in the morning when a fire truck passes by.

And all right, it isn't really singing, it's howling. But people call it singing, and they lap it up if your dog can do it on cue. In fact, an even better party trick is to announce that you're going to do a duet, and then *you* sing along with him.

Unfortunately, some dogs are more difficult to train than others. Although wolves frequently sing, some dogs can't be trained at all. A Doberman will probably not sing; a sled or northern dog probably will; a poodle might; and a New Guinea singing dog can be trained not only to sing but to harmonize on cue.

There's also an occasional dog whose owner swears can sing a special tune, like the Samoyed in England named Basil who can sing "My Way." Let's hope we'll never have to hear it.

If you think your dog doesn't have it in him to sing, trainer Captain Haggerty, from Los Angeles, says you can do it if you start by singing some very high notes. Alternately, you can try playing them— on the piano, a soprano recorder, from a tape recording of a siren sound, a harmonica, or an ocarina—until you find a note that makes your dog respond.

While you're doing this, Haggerty, who also acts and writes books, suggests you croon "sing, sing, sing" in a rising tone, and keep repeating it. Some dogs will react to the high-pitched sound.

Then, one second after your dog is finished singing, give him a verbal and physical reward. Make a big fuss over him, and then follow it up with food so it's one big flowing reward.

He says timing is critical. If you give your dog a food reward the minute he starts to sing, not only do you break his concentration, but he'll stop singing to get the food. You also have to hope that in the future, he doesn't start howling when he's hungry as a way of saying "Where's my food?"

An advantage to a duet is that you can usually keep your dog going longer. Howling is generally of short duration unless you sing along, too. But singing along is also a way to get him to stop. He'll probably keep singing as long as you do—or as long as you play the pitch he likes.

Therefore, if you stop singing, and say "performance ended," people will be impressed, thinking he's responding to what you said. If he still won't stop, give him a sharp "no." But be careful, because this could stop him permanently from doing any further arias with you.

If you want your little routine to be a howling success, Captain Haggerty suggests that at the end you hang a small basket from your dog's mouth and announce that he accepts tips. Or teach him how to take a bow, which you can learn how to do from a book he cowrote with Carol Lea Benjamin, entitled *Dog Tricks*.

60 Diseases You Can Catch
from Your Dog–and
6 You Can Give Him

There are only a few diseases that you can give your pet, but unfortunately your canine can make *you* sicker than a dog. In many different ways, dogs can transmit—directly or indirectly—up to three hundred diseases to man. So let's start with the much shorter list of problems people can give to their pooches. Zoonotic expert Dr. James B. Miller lists **tuberculosis, streptococcus infections,** and, indirectly, **Lyme disease**—and **plague**. The last would be highly unlikely, since people with plague are so sick, they're in a hospital where there would be no contact with dogs' fleas.

Dr. George D. Whitney, author of *The Complete Book of Dog Care*, which includes a chapter on zoonotic diseases, added **athlete's foot** and **ringworm,** saying that the latter can be transmitted back and forth between man and dog.

Now, on to the much larger group of diseases your dog can—but probably won't—give you. Most of the following problems can be easily cured, and pose little long-term threat to healthy people. Those most at risk are generally the elderly and immune-compromised.

That doesn't mean that healthy younger people can ignore them, however. A few of these diseases may start out in a mild, and treatable, form, but if undiagnosed and/or ignored, can go on to cause extreme problems, or even death. Since some of these diseases are rare in this country, it's important if you're sick that you tell your doctor if you've been out of the country, especially in some exotic locale.

One problem for doctors, though, is that the symptoms of some zoonotic diseases are similar to those of other diseases, and since the suspicion for dog-transmitted diseases tends to be low, there have been some tragic misdiagnoses.

277 Secrets Your Dog Wants You to Know

For example, some **worms** can cause symptoms that have sometimes been confused with cancer. (A severe **heartworm infection** has been mistaken for lung cancer.) A spirochete infection from a swimming hole contaminated by dog's feces once led to an erroneous diagnosis of polio in a group of boys. Confusion may also arise with salmonella symptoms, which can resemble typhoid fever. Or **toxocariasis**, a parasitic larvae that lodges in the eye, which can lead to the removal of an eye if a doctor doesn't know what it is. All this, however, is rare.

So is the possibility of getting any of the following diseases from your dog. Happily, "simple hygiene procedures can prevent almost all of them," promises Dr. Miller. Dr. Miller helped put together the following list, which is also based on *The Merck Veterinary Manual;* plus a paper by James H. Steele, D.V.M., professor emeritus at the University of Texas Health Science Center; the book *Pets and Your Health* by Drs. Kevin Cahill and William O'Brien; and an article in the October 17, 1986, issue of *The New England Journal of Medicine,* co-written by Dr. Miller.

Flea allergy dermatitis, dog tapeworm, fish tapeworm, and **plague** can partially be avoided by keeping your dog free of fleas. Ticks and mosquitoes present other problems, so check your dog carefully and keep him sprayed or dipped to protect him and you from getting diseases like **Rocky Mountain spotted fever, tularemia, acariasis, filariasis, arbovirus, piroplasmosis, tick paralysis**, or **Lyme disease**. Also, **dirofilariasis** (heartworm) may be passed on to humans via mosquitoes, resulting in chest lesions and other pulmonary problems. So keep up your dog's heartworm medication.

As for dog bites, **rabies** is the number one problem here, although other possible dangers include **tetanus** and **pasteurella multocida**.

Parks where children play are often areas where dogs also play, although backyards can harbor dangerous organisms if dogs relieve themselves there. More commonly, children touch the ground, which may be contaminated, and then put their fingers and other objects in their mouths. This exposes them to many diseases through urine and feces. Gardeners and farmers are also at risk.

One familiar problem is **ringworm**, which, incidentally, isn't a worm but a fungal disease, and the lesions aren't always ring-shaped. Another danger is **roundworm**. A young child who contracts this may start out with a simple squint, and ultimately lose an eye. There's also **hookworm** or creeping eruption, characterized by inflamed and irritating red lines under the surface of their skin. **Coenuriasis,** a parasitic worm disease that can infect humans if they accidentally swallow contaminated eggs, can lead to a brain tumor.

Here's more: A common fluke parasite causes **schistomiasis**. Dogs' droppings may carry **salmonella**. Bacterial infections include **brucellosis** which is found in the genitourinary secretions of dogs. Also, **leptospirosis** comes from the urine, blood or tissues of infected stray dogs. And we hear more these days about **cat scratch fever, campylobacteriosis,** and **giardiasis**.

Adding to this list, Dr. Steven Radbill says dogs can give people **pseudomonas infections**, and Dr. George D. Whitney wrote that people who eat rare dog might get **trichinosis**. (Serves them right.)

Whitney also believes that **poison ivy** may be contracted by dogs who have been running in the woods, and then transferred to people when they touch their own skin after petting the dog.

If you haven't had enough yet, here are a few more zoonotic diseases you probably don't have to worry about: **dipylidiasis, tunga infections, pentastomid infections, topocariosis, choriomeningitis, hydatid disease, hymenolepiasis, murine typhus, boutonneuse fever, sporotrichosis, nocardiosis, blastomycosis, strongyloidiasis, thelaziasis, hirudiniasis, rhinosporidiosis, capillariasis, clonorchiasis, cutaneous larva migrans, visceral larva, giant kidney worm, gnathostomiasis, dracunculiasis, echinostromiasis, fasciolopsiasis, metagonimiasis, pisthorchiasis, parasoniamiasis, chagas disease,** and **coccidiosis cryptospordiosis.**

If you're getting worried about all this, here are some more things you can do to protect yourself and your children from zoonotic diseases.

1. Maintain rigid adherence to pooper-scooper laws.

2. Keep dogs out of playgrounds.

3. Have your children wash their hands frequently.

4. Make sure dog feces are disposed of properly, not just slightly buried.

5. Puppies must be dewormed at two weeks of age.

6. Don't let dogs ingest stool.

7. Don't let your dogs roam about, especially in parks, playgrounds, and on beaches.

8. Keep your dogs' nails trimmed.

9. Always supervise your children's play areas.

10. Wash your dogs' feeding bowls and utensils separately from yours.

11. Watch out for that old swimming hole! It may have been great in the movies, or your memory, but be wary of water shared with dogs.

12. Keep all vaccinations up to date.

13. Report all unusual symptoms to your doctor.

9 "People" Foods You Should
Never Feed Your Dog

Even if *you're* careful about what foods you give your dog, he may steal something from a table, counter, or garbage container. Regardless of how he obtains it, the following foods, either originally intended for people, or given to a dog by people, can cause severe—in some cases even fatal—reactions in dogs. Dr. Ernest Poortinga, D.V.M., a veterinary poison information specialist for the University of Illinois's National Animal Poison Control Center discusses them.

Chocolate: Valentine's Day, Christmas, and the Fourth of July may not be happy holidays for your pets. Indeed, many emergency visits to vets are from dogs who ate the candy intended for their owners.

Chocolates contain varying levels of caffeine and a similar compound called theobromine, which can have serious effects on a dog's heart and central nervous system. How much is too much? It depends on the type and the dog. A single milk chocolate bar (approximately 1.6 ounces) eaten by a 10-pound dog could cause adverse reactions. But the ingestion of the same amount of unsweetened baker's chocolate—which contains ten times as much caffeine and theobromine as milk chocolate—could kill the same dog. In South Bend, Indiana, it was reported that a dog died after eating only one bag of chocolate-coated peanut butter cups.

Onions: The only thing worse for your dog than stealing your Chicken with 40 Cloves of Garlic would be if he got into the bag of fried onion rings you were going to serve with it. Onions and garlic have high levels of a sulphur compound that in large amounts can cause damage to red blood cells. This often results in hemolytic anemia and there is no evidence that cooking removes this compound.

Moldy refrigerated foods: Some people give their dogs cheese or sour cream that has become moldy, instead of disposing of it; or

Will Alcohol or Marijuana Harm Your Dog?

A dog won't be harmed by alcohol in moderation, like a half a bottle of beer for an average-sized dog, according to Dr. Steven Radbill. But he cautions that beer is fattening, so if your dog is overweight, keep him on the wagon.

That will probably be easy, because dogs generally don't like the taste of alcohol, unless they were fed it as puppies. So they're unlikely to raid your liquor cabinet and take a snort of their own.

Then how about a marijuana brownie? Actually, the chocolate in the brownie might hurt him more than the marijuana. Although in larger quantities it may cause depression or hyperactivity, vomiting, and respiratory problems, in small quantities, "Marijuana is not bad for dogs in the sense that it will harm them," says Dr. Radbill, coauthor of *The Complete Book of Questions Dog Owners Ask Their Vet and Answers.* "But, like people, it would probably make them lose some of their judgment.

"Dogs can act very bizarre under it," he continues. "People call me in the middle of the night and don't say what happened, but I know what is going on, because they say their dog has fallen out of the bed, is acting really weird, vocalizing, and the dog's eyes are dilated."

Still, he says marijuana isn't a good idea for dogs *psychologically* because "the dog doesn't realize what's happening to him. Cats wouldn't have as strong a reaction because they're used to their catnip."

dogs may fish it out of the garbage on their own after their owner has thrown it out. But many moldy foods that have been refrigerated can cause profound muscle tremors and seizures. One terrier-Pekingese mix died after he ate overripe Roquefort cheese.

Moldy walnuts can be a source of the same toxin, Penitrem A, produced by a fungus, and found in moldy dairy products.

Chicken or turkey bones: By now, dog owners generally know that chicken bones are dangerous because they're so small and sharp. But they mistakenly assume turkey bones are safe. These can also pierce a dog's esophagus.

Beef or pork bones: The tiny "spicules" or small, sharp pieces of bones that dogs swallow while gnawing on the bones can be very

Why Do Dogs Watch Us Eat?

Some people think their dog is so cute when he watches them eat, waiting for his little scraps. But some behaviorists say the dog isn't being cute at all; he's passively/aggressively trying to stare them down. A few have also theorized that he may not be waiting to be *handed* scraps—but for them to be regurgitated for him, as his mother did for him. Some cute.

abrasive to the lining of their gastrointestinal tract. They can also bind together like cement, causing complete or partial obstruction.

Raw or undercooked meat: Forget the old days when people threw a slab of raw meat at a dog and everyone was happy. Nowadays, you've got to worry about salmonella, *E. coli*, and risks from other food-borne bacteria. Cook meat thoroughly; neither of you should eat hamburger unless it's gray or brown inside, and the juice is clear rather than red.

Greasy table scraps: Even people who know not to give a dog the turkey bones may give him the skin, or let him lick the grease off some cooking pan. Frequent eating of fat can lead to obesity—but even a single ingestion of this type of food can trigger a life-threatening inflammation of the pancreas.

Salt: Some people attempt to use salt to induce vomiting in a dog they think has been poisoned. Only two grams of salt (less than ½ teaspoon) per pound of body weight is considered lethal to dogs.

If you have any questions about anything your dog has eaten, call the National Animal Poison Control Center, a nonprofit organization located at the College of Veterinary Medicine at the University of Illinois, at (800) 548-2423. It costs $30 (major credit cards accepted) for as many calls as the case requires.

For quick questions, or if you don't have a credit card, call their other number, (900) 680-0000. It costs $20 for the first five minutes and $2.95 for each additional minute. Some manufacturers will pay for consultations involving exposure to their products, so call the 800 line first to see if there will be a charge.

How to Get Your Dog into Show Business

Perhaps you've been watching a commercial in which a dog scratches his fleas and you've been thinking, "Heck, my dog does that all day long at home for free." The difference is this: that dog doesn't have any fleas. He's probably been trained to scratch himself when his owner does the same thing off-camera.

Whether your canine could become a celebrity depends upon his appearance, abilities, and both your temperament and his. Here are a few other things you should know:

- Don't be a stage mama. You may be scrutinized as carefully as your animal at an audition. Barbara Austin, president of the Dawn Animal Agency in Manhattan, explains that since they often send the owner out to a shoot, they look for people who are quiet, intelligent, poised, and don't seem overanxious.

- Don't worry if your pet is older. The first Benji was cast at 10½ and was almost 14 by the time the movie was made. The only sure disqualification for your dog is if he's black. Cinematographer Lenny Hirschfield says they don't film black dogs because it's too hard to see their features against a light background.

- If you want your dog to do commercials, sitcoms, television shows or movies, it's better to live in New York or the greater Los Angeles area, where most are produced. It's also easier to attend auditions, callbacks, and last-minute rehearsals. But if you live elsewhere, your dog may still find work appearing in local advertising and catalogues—which may lead to bigger things.

The 10 Best Dog Movies on Video

Since the early twenties, when German shepherd Rin Tin Tin kept the foundering, nearly bankrupt Warner Bros. Studio above water, and Asta outfoxed Nick and Nora in *The Thin Man* series, movie producers have often turned to canines to take a bite out of the viewer's wallet at the box office.

Each of the following pictures is available for home video rental; some may also be obtainable for purchase. The titles are alphabetical. We have not included pictures in which the dog is only a supporting player (*The Thin Man, Down and Out in Beverly Hills, The Wizard of Oz*) or the villain (*Cujo*).

All Dogs Go to Heaven (animated, 1989, MGM)

Beethoven (Charles Grodin, Dean Jones, 1992, MCA)

Benji (1973, Vestron & others)

Dog of Flanders (David Ladd, Donald Crisp, Theodore Bikel, 1959, Paramount)

The Incredible Journey (1963, Disney)

Lady and the Tramp (animated, 1955, Disney)

Lassie Come Home (Roddy McDowall, Elizabeth Taylor, 1943, MGM)

Old Yeller (Dorothy McGuire, Fess Parker, 1957, Disney)

101 Dalmatians (animated, 1961, Disney)

The Shaggy Dog (Fred MacMurray, Jean Hagen, 1959, Disney)

• Many places prefer that you and your dog have gone to a recognized obedience training school. Together, of course!

• Don't turn Rover into a robot. "Stop training your dog if you think he's losing his own personality, becoming too rigid, or looking over at you too often for cues," says Austin. She says producers dislike robotic, overtrained animals because it may be hard to get them to follow the commands they want.

Top Dogs on Today's TV Sitcoms

FRASIER: "Eddie," the three-year-old Jack Russell terrier on *Frasier,* is really named "Moose." He belonged to a couple who placed him for adoption after they moved to California. He is the proud father of three puppies with "Mrs. Moose," a stand-in for "Eddie" on the show.

MAD ABOUT YOU: Murray's real name is "Maui" and he's a five-year-old collie mix rescued from an animal shelter by his trainer.

DAVE'S WORLD: Ernest was a rescue dog for eight years when *she* was adopted from a shelter. She's eleven years old now, and among her many tricks, she can take on an "amused look."

MARRIED WITH CHILDREN: This eleven-year-old briard is today's longest lasting canine television star. "Buck's" tricks include waving and looking stunned, and it has been said that he has turned lying down into an art form.

Thanks to Wayne Grover, author of children's animal books, who researched this material for the *National Enquirer.*

- Look up "Animal Rental" in the yellow pages, or *Kemps International Film & Television Year Book.* Send each agency a description of your dog and his training, along with a good head shot, plus another photo of your dog performing a task.

- Don't tranquilize your dog before an audition or shoot because it can cause unexpected reactions. If your dog can't respond correctly in one take in a strange environment, with people milling and shouting around him, other animals standing temptingly in front of him, and lights flashing or focusing at him, find another career for your dog.

- If you're angling for a dog food commercial, give your dog some of the product for a few days before the casting so he won't reject it. If he doesn't like it at first, introduce it to him slowly so he's salivating at the audition.

- Forget the "grunge" look for your dog. Photogenic dogs are generally chosen over dogs with other qualities.

- Learn how the business operates. If you want your dog to be a star, or even a spokespet for a product, know the difference between the producer, the casting director, and the agent. There are good books on the subject.

- You don't need a purebred to succeed. It's true that pedigrees—especially dalmatians, Jack Russell terriers, and golden retrievers—are currently in demand for fashion and advertising that implies taste, cultivation, and above-average income. But mixed breeds are more often shown with kids, in all-American settings, or in catalogues with less expensive items.

- Don't expect to get rich. Animal agencies siphon off a hefty but well-deserved commission. Payment for a day on a film is about $450. There are no residuals because animals don't have unions. Print and ad work pays about $150. Catalogue work around $125 an hour. Television commercials pay about $325. Runway work, in which your dog gets held by a model, is supposed to be about $75 an hour. But according to Atlanta models, Darryl B. Cohen, Esq. and Tracy White, dogs usually aren't paid at all, but rather contributed by their owners for the exposure.

- Don't expect overnight success. Today's understudy can be tomorrow's star. Indeed, the first Lassie, in the 1943 version, was a stand-in who was later picked for the lead. And be prepared for disappointment. Your dog only has about a 200-to-1 chance of being chosen because the competition is so beastly.

How to Tell What Your Dog Is Thinking by Looking at His Tail (and 13 Things a Wagging Tail Can Really Mean)

It was once written in a fortune cookie, "A dog is a good friend—he wags his tail and not his tongue." Most of us enjoy seeing a dog wag his tail because we assume it means the dog is happy. But is that true?

It would appear that a dog is trying to say *something* when he does it, because he only wags at living objects with whom he can communicate. Although he may be happy to see his food or his ball, he no more wags his tail at them than most of us talk to brick walls.

So what is he saying when his tail starts swaying? It depends on his ears, face, the speed of the wag, the position of the tail, the mast, whether it's been docked, the type of dog it is, the circumstances, and which behaviorist is analyzing it. For example, by wagging his tail, your dog could be telling you:

1. I'm interested in what you're saying.

2. I don't understand you but I'm trying to.

3. I'm in a rotten mood so go away.

4. I'm nervous.

5. I'm no good.

6. I may attack.

7. I *really* don't like you.

8. Hello.

9. I like you.

10. I'm excited.

11. I want to play.

12. I see you looking at me.

13. I'm anxious.

Your Dog's Eyes Tell What's Happening in His Head

Dogs watch our eyes when they look at us, because eye contact is an important means of communicating authority. Direct stares are a challenge; dominant dogs stare down lesser ones. Conversely, dogs who avoid eye contact may be submissive, anxious to avoid confrontations; in short, "pet-rified."

When a dog's eyes are partially closed, it may signal cowardliness and suspicion. Wide-opened eyes mean they want to play—or fight, depending on what else is going on in their body or surroundings at the time.

How can you tell? Generally, the higher the mouth is raised, the greater the degree of aggression. "Any curled lip should be taken seriously," says animal behaviorist and author Warren Eckstein.

Of course, dogs do much more with their tails than just wag them. Many well-known American, Canadian, and English animal behaviorists, including Stanley Coren, Ian Dunbar, Warren Eckstein, Michael W. Fox, Jean George, Desmond Morris, and Barbara Woodhouse, among others, have written about the meaning of the positions of a dog's tail, which at times seems to reflect the dog's mental state, what's likely to happen next, and the dog's social standing.

Most agree that a dog in a tail-down position is probably undergoing some kind of insecurity, as if saying, "I'm not too sure about this." Keeping his tail down also shows subordination, appeasement, and reduced status, since dogs who are lower-ranking hold their heads and tails lower when they meet superior dogs.

But, if a dog keeps his tail down, he can also be saying "I'm afraid, don't hurt me," especially when his tail is curled and tucked between the legs. Desmond Morris writes that when a dog does this, the cringing animal is effectively cutting off his scent signals, the canine equivalent of an insecure person hiding his face.

So, the next time you walk your dog and come upon another dog, watch to see what each one does with his tail. If yours raises it, he may be trying to establish dominance. If he lowers it, he's conceding that the other is the top dog. But if either dog points his tail

3 Ideas from Roger Caras

We had a wonderful chat with Roger Caras, the dean of dog writers, author of seventy pet and wildlife books, voice of major televised canine competitions, and president of the American Society for the Prevention of Cruelty to Animals in New York. Here are a few of the many interesting things he said:

- When you see a handler at the Westminster Show slipping a dog something from a plastic bag in his pocket, it's probably a piece of dried liver. The handler took a slab of liver, put it on a cookie sheet until it was dry, and broke it into inch or so pieces. It is the ultimate. Dogs adore it.

- I'm trying to get people to call mixed breeds "random breed dogs" so then there will be purebred and random bred dogs. It gives them a little more dignity.

- There are dogs who are superbright but can drive you crazy trying to train them, because they're too highly motivated in other directions. I have a Border collie, who is the son of the one in *Down and Out in Beverly Hills*. He is the most difficult dog I've ever owned out of sixty or seventy.

   He's bright as hell but he's so exceedingly powerfully motivated that he can't control himself. I can take a far more placid dog and teach it anything except calculus and it won't be as bright, but it will be attentive and want to learn.

straight out away from his body, horizontal to the ground, be careful—especially if the fur on his neck and/or back starts to bristle. The dog may be wondering which one is boss—and attack the other to establish that issue.

15 Unusual Gifts You Can Buy Your Dog (and Yourself)

1. **If your dog likes to mount furniture and people's legs**... you might want to buy the new Humpy-Toy. (Or you might want to *train* your dog instead!) The owner touts this as the answer to oversexed dogs with "the urge to merge." It's a long, fluffy hot dog-shaped pillow a dog can—if not sink its teeth into—at least wrap his legs around. Available from Lorin's Pet Supply.

2. **If you've always wanted to communicate telepathically with your dog**... try the Telepathic Communication with Animals video. Forty-six minutes of scenery, music, and subliminal messages to help you solve your dog's behavior problems, find out where he hurts, and discover his likes and dislikes. Available from Direct Book Service, in Wenatchee, Washington.

3. **Every dog needs his very own gumball machine—or does he?** The Doggie Treat-Machine may not be the world's most indispensable item, but it sure is one of the stranger ones. Teach your dog to pull a lever from the machine and out comes his treat. Now, how do you teach him to stop doing it? Available from Sam & Sally Creature Comforts.

4. **Now your dog can ring a bell if he wants to go out**. We don't know if this is ridiculous or an absolutely great idea. The Doggie Doorbell hangs over a door, looking like a fireplug or tree. There are bells on it, which your dog can hit with his paws or his nose when he wants to go out. Available from Roberta K. Frush Enterprises.

5. **Or if he'd prefer to use the bathroom in your house**.... This is for real! A Walk-Me-Not dog toilet that rolls into place

Do Electronic Flea Collars Work?

Not according to veterinarian and writer Bonnie Wilcox. In her monthly column in *Dog Fancy*, she reported that there was little data to substantiate claims that they do work. In fact, studies have shown that they *don't* "repel fleas, affect jumping rates, interfere with reproduction, or alter development of fleas," says the Milan, Illinois, doctor.

What they may do is disturb your dog, because of the high-frequency sound emitted by the collars. *Dog Fancy's* advice: don't buy one unless you get a money-back guarantee.

over your toilet so you won't have to walk your dog anymore. He just walks on and it even self flushes upon completion.

6. **"Good Gollie Miss Collie," "Boogie Woogie Beagle Boy," and "Something Smug about a Pug"**—These are three of sixty breed songs available that characterize the style, personality and talents of a particular breed. Available from Direct Book Service.

7. **If your dog likes to watch television,** he'll love the "Happy Tails" video. Filmed from a dog's eye view, it's got scenes that dogs will like: fields, farms, and other dogs. Available from Paw Print Video Productions.

8. **If you can't remember to buy your dog a gift each month...**then why not enroll him in the Dog Treat of the Month Club? Each month, your dog will get a gift-wrapped bag of all-natural, handmade doggy treats decorated according to the season or holiday. Available from Unique Concepts.

9. **Every well-dressed dog must have her nails done.** And she can have a choice of twenty colors, including fuchsia, gold, silver sparkle, hot pink, and white. Quick-drying for those last-minute touch-ups she may need. The minimum order from R. C Steele is $50, so you'll have to send for their catalogue and see if there are any doggie clothes to go with her nails.

10. **If your dog tries to get away when you're bathing him,** Bath Helper holds him so you can use both hands for washing.

You attach the suction cup to the bathtub wall, and your dog to the suction cup with the chew-resistant cable. Available from Pedigrees in Brockport, NY.

11. **Here's the latest scoop on doggie poop.** Picking up after your dog is neighbor- and environment-friendly, and just out is an easy way to do it. Petmitts are disposable plastic mittens: you slip one on your hand, pick up the waste, pull the cuff over your hand, twist the mitt with a tie, and dispose of it. What could be better—except a dog that would pick up after itself? Each box contains 100 mitts and 100 twist ties. Available from Petmitts.

12. **Your little angel should also look like one.** A heavenly gift of attachable wings and a halo for your dog. In small or large size. Available from Discount Master Animal Care, in Hazelton, PA.

13. **Does your pooch have a paunch?** Buy him a doggie treadmill, which is great even for thin dogs who need a lot of exercise. Jog-A-Dog is a motorized treadmill that comes in three sizes—and it's for real. Available from Jog-A-Dog.

14. **Now where has that dog gone?** You know your dog is going on the carpet when you're not around, but you're not sure exactly where and so you can't use odor remover to deter him from returning to the spot. Nature's Miracle Blacklite, a 1½-foot-long unit, plugs into a wall socket; when you shine it on the carpet, it lights up the protein in the dog's urine. You might feel like a fool crawling around the floor with this contraption, but if this will solve your problem, go for it.

15. **Let your dog give you something on your birthday.** We loved the Canine Chorus, a group of dogs that sing-bark "Happy Birthday" in fifties, country, and blues styles, and more. (They also make one with cats.) Available from Buff Enterprises.

NOTE: some mail order companies selling items for dogs go out of business and catalogue houses stop stocking items. Also, some of these items may also be available at the larger chain pet department stores such as Petco, Petsmart, and Petstuff.

Ordering Information

1. Lorin's Pet Supply, P.O. Box 1432, Estero, FL 33928. $15 + $5 s/h.

2. Direct Book Service. (800) 776-2665. $29.95 + $5.50 s/h. #DTB227.

3. Sam & Sally Creature Comforts, P.O. Box 1694, Center City, MN 55012. $39.95 + $4 s/h.

4. Roberta K. Frush Enterprises, 341 Chestnut Circle, Winthrop Harbor, IL 60096. $24.95 + $4 s/h.

5. Richard P. Wooten, P.O. Box 1175, Lanham, MD 20703. $900.

6. Direct Book Service. (800) 776-2665. $9.95 ea. + $3.95 s/h.

7. Paw Print Video Productions, P.O. Box 55071, 1800 Sheppard Ave., East Willowdale, Ontario, Canada. $14.99 (U.S.) and $19.99 (Canada).

8. Unique Concepts, 1559 LaSalle, Chicago, IL 60610. $51.51 for 6 mo.

9. R.C. Steele. (800) 872-3773. $1.98 ea., 3 or more $1.84 ea.

10. Pedigrees. (800) 548-4786. $10.99 + $4.99 s/h.

11. Petmitts. P.O. Box 541613, Dallas, TX 75354. (800) PET-MITT. $16.95 incl. s/h.

12. Discount Master Animal Care. (800) 346-0749. $9.99 + s/h.

13. Jog-A-Dog. (800) 756-4364. $995–$1820.

14. New England Serum Company & Wholesale Pet U.S.A. (800) 637-3786. $29.93 + $3.00 s/h.

15. Buff Enterprises, P.O. Box 917, Ansonia Station, New York, NY 10023. $6 + $1.50 s/h.

Would Prozac Help
Your Dog?

Is your dog dejected? Is your canine compulsively scratching himself? Since we live in a Prozac Nation, and our dogs live here with us, it was inevitable that we'd share our Prozac with them, too. We've given drugs like Valium to dogs for years, so why not antidepressants?

Many vets are asking, "Why not?" The *Wall Street Journal* interviewed several who said Prozac *did* help their dogs' behavior problems. They may not see many alternatives. Many people with "mutt cases" on their hands don't want or can't afford to go to dog behaviorists and psychologists. Furthermore, the latter don't always succeed, perhaps because most dogs enjoy lying on a couch, but they can't tell anyone about their mothers.

Seriously, dog depression is one problem for which Prozac is being prescribed. ("What do dogs have to be depressed about?" asks one critic. "Isn't it supposed to be a dog's life?") Vets report that Prozac does work for this. But as one woman told *Newsweek* of her Prozac-drugged dog, "She sleeps all the time anyway, so it's hard to see much change in her behavior."

The second problem for which Prozac is frequently being prescribed is dogs constantly licking, scratching, biting, or chewing the same spot. Dogs who do this—sometimes for hours—usually concentrate on their front or hind feet, or "wrist" joints, often creating a "hot spot" or lick granuloma there.

The problem is probably psychological, possibly corresponding to human obsessive-compulsive disorders. After all, a compulsive dog can't wash his hands ten times before he eats, or check the door a dozen times to see if it's locked after he goes out.

"We focus more on the brain because we feel that that's where it starts," says William Fortney, D.V.M. "What follows is a resultant

Pampered Pets of Japan

Ever dream of a luxury wedding and honeymoon weekend at a gorgeous resort in Japan, complete with bubble bath and a relaxing treatment in hot sand?

It's available—but not for you. For $300 a day, sick or overweight dogs are sent to this Japanese spa, where they're buried up to their necks in steaming sand, receive beauty treatments, and learn to do yoga!

Elsewhere in Japan, according to the *National Enquirer*, they also know how to treat a dog like a king. They offer a combination wedding-honeymoon weekend with private reception and doggy bubble bath. When the honeymoon is over, the happy canine couple can live in their $9,000 doghouse with a VCR containing animal videos. And for their first anniversary, they can go off to a doggy hotel, where the $165 room comes with twenty-four-hour animal movies, snacks of fancy French food—plus American style barbecues.

And you thought *your* dog was spoiled!

problem in the foot or wrist." He says they've tried Prozac at Kansas State University, where he's from, but they don't give it except in special circumstances. "We feel other drugs work better for conditions such as these."

We found older veterinary journals filled with supposedly successful treatments for this problem. The latest articles tout radiation, but in the past, chemotherapy, acupuncture, and even cobra venom have given some of these dogs a whole new leash on life.

So, does your dog really need Prozac? (If you're taking it, by the way, the dosage is different so don't give him yours.) According to Dr. Dennis O'Brien, professor of veterinary neurology at the University of Missouri, Prozac *is* safe and effective—but training may work just as well.

Or there's always that couch.

Your Dog Could Be Allergic to You

Some dogs develop a strong allergic reaction to a particular person. Irwin Small, D.V.M., asserts that it isn't psychological; it's a physiological response to some protein in the person's skin. "We talk about pheromones, which are secreted chemical substances, and these can be repulsing as well as attractive," he says.

Unfortunately, if the allergy is severe, the person may have to get rid of his or her dog. Dr. Small says it's possible to give dogs corticosteroids for this problem, but "in the long term, these drugs can cause a lot of problem in the adrenal glands."

What Does Your Dog
Think About All Day?

Ever wonder what your dog thinks of—and thinks of you? Here are some opinions on that:

A dog thinks about food and sex.

      —ROGER CARAS on the *Bertice Berry* show

We ourselves live a good deal in the past; we have visions, pleasant or unpleasant, regarding the future.... The dog on the other hand is very unlikely to dwell on past happenings unless one has made a deep impression, such as a whipping. It has no anticipation of the future and is content to enjoy the present to the full....

    Man also lives in terror of dying. Dogs, like other animals, have no knowledge of death.... It does not realize as the years pass that it is growing old and will shortly leave this world.

      —R.H. SMYTHE, M.R.C.V.S.,
      The Private Life of the Dog

They sit around, they follow the owner going "Mmmm, ooop, happy, sad, angry," all right? They read us better than we read them. What else do they have to do all day? They don't watch the news.

      —BRIAN KILCOMMONS on ABC News *20-20*

Ever consider what they must think of us? I mean, here we come back from a grocery store with the most amazing haul—chicken, pork, half a cow.... They must think we're the greatest hunters on earth!

      —ANN TYLER quoted in *Mondo Canine*

Cupid for Single Dog Owners

Unmarried...with dog? Looking for a similarly situated companion? *Dog Lover's Junction* is a bimonthly newsletter presenting personal notices with a canine-oriented perspective.

Here are some sample lines from actual ads:

- SEEKING FEMALE WHO DOESN'T MIND DOG HAIR IN THE HOUSE.

- THE THING I LOVE MOST ABOUT DOGS IS THEIR UNCONDITIONAL LOVE. WOULD LOVE TO FIND A WOMAN WITH THAT SAME TRAIT.

- IF LOOKS ARE NOT THE MOST IMPORTANT THING ABOUT PEOPLE OR DOGS TO YOU, WE...MAY BE ABLE TO SEE THE BEAUTY OF HUMAN AND CANINE INNER SELVES.

- SEEKING WOMAN WHO WON'T BE JEALOUS OF MY RELATIONSHIP WITH MY DOG.

- HAVE DOGS (MIXED BREED SPANIELS) THAT THINK THEY'RE HUNTING DOGS BUT REALLY AREN'T.

- ALSO LOVE CATS, BUT MY DOG DOESN'T.

- SEEKING A WOMAN WHO SPENDS A MINIMUM OF 10 HOURS A WEEK WITH HER DOG.

For more information, write to Dog Lover's Junction, P.O. Box 4767, Silver Spring, MD 20914.

From the dog's point of view, his master is an elongated and abnormally cunning dog.

    —MABEL LOUISE ROBINSON quoted in *Mondo Canine*

Lie flat on the floor and have someone stand over you. Strange feeling isn't it? This gives you an idea of what Fido sees.... People who are upset, possibly correcting or scolding him.... Even people who are friendly look something like the Jolly Green Giant.

    —WARREN ECKSTEIN, *How to Get Your Dog to Do What You Want*

Why Not a Take-Your-Dog-to-the-Office Day?

Take-Your-Daughter-to-Work Day has inspired a similar one for sons. But wouldn't it be nice if they expanded this into a Take-Your-Dog-to-the-Office Day? That way, people could see that most dogs were not disruptive to job performance, and could actually enhance it—as well as increase the camaraderie among the employees. Then soon all of us could take our dogs to work all the time!

It's already happening in some places, and interest is growing. An article on dogs going to the office has just appeared in the *AKC Gazette*, and that may start the ball rolling.

They pointed out that many owners of one-person offices are doing it, along with a few store owners. Those they interviewed believed that having their dog in their store resulted in increased sales and reduced burglaries.

Next thing you know, our dogs will be asking for social security and dogman's compensation.

You are much larger than your dog is. When he looks up at you he sees an overpowering figure with huge, tentacle-like fingers wiggling in a threatening manner, getting ready to pick him up and hug him to death.

— MORDECAI SIEGAL AND MATTHEW MARGOLIS,
Good Dog, Bad Dog

We seem to understand our animals quite a bit better if we accept the fact that they have simple feelings, fears, desires, and beliefs, make plans, have goals, and the like. How can anyone live with a dog without thinking, "The dog is thirsty and wants some water," when it stands over an empty water dish, barks, and then pushes it toward you with its nose?

— STANLEY COREN, *The Intelligence of Dogs*

How to Save Your Dog's Life
in a Plane Crash

Each year hundreds of thousands of people travel with small pets in the cabin with them, but the safety instructions never include how to save *them* in a crash. Most flight attendants won't tell you the truth either, because the best things you can do to save your dog go against airline procedure.

But here's what three flight attendants (from TWA, USAir, and Continental) told us off the record that they would do if their dog was with them in a crate under the seat, and they had time to prepare for a crash landing.

One recommended that even before you fly, try to book the aisle seat right behind an exit row. You can't be in the exit row itself because there's no seat directly in front of you in which to stow the crate. Then, when you get on board, pay extra attention to the safety procedures, because saving your dog will make it more difficult for you to escape and you'll need every bit of help you can get.

When you put the crate under the seat in front of you, the opening clasp should face you. If the crate only fits sideways, and you're right-handed, face the clasp to the right (or to the left if you're a lefty), so you can open it faster.

If you realize you're going down, with your seat belt still on, if you have time, regardless of the airline rules, the attendants recommend you immediately pull the dog's crate out from under the seat, and take the dog out. Why not leave him under the seat? First, you may only have a few seconds to get yourself out later, possibly with smoke and flames around you. Also say you're in the middle or aisle seat. As one attendant told us, "After a plane crashes, if I'm bending down and tugging and pulling on a crate, the others next to me might trample me trying to get out."

Would You Give Up Your Dog for 1 Million Dollars?

We conducted a little survey in New York, asking ten women and ten men walking their dogs if they would give them up for one million dollars. Four of the men said yes. A few of the women hesitated, but in the end, only one would take the million dollars. Those who wouldn't give up their dogs said things like:

> *"When I only had my papillon for two weeks, I wouldn't have given it up for a million dollars."*
>
> —BONNIE BROWN, real estate agent

> *"I wouldn't give mine up for ten million dollars."*
>
> —ROBIN STELTEN, of Palm Springs, therapist

> *"You've got to be kidding—my dog got me through my divorce."*
>
> —MARION SHAPIRO, teacher

> *"When my husband said he wanted to get rid of our 'baby,' I said 'you go first.'"*
>
> —HAIRDRESSER, who withheld her name

And one man who refused to give his name said, "I would give my wife up for one million dollars but never my dog."

Also, try to put the empty crate back under the seat before you land, or it's a potential hazard that could make it more difficult to escape as well as get in a crash-land position. As for your dog, one attendant suggested that if the seat next to you is empty, try to put the seat belt around him. Otherwise, put him on your lap. They thought the best crash position then was leaning forward, with your hand on the back of the seat in front of you.

Finally, when you get to the slide, fold your arms with your dog inside and slide. If you send him down first, the waiting attendants may toss him aside to free their hands, and he could disappear, run away, or wait for you at the bottom of the chute and be hit as you slide down.

One last thing: several airlines that permit dogs in the cabin now allow owners to carry their dogs in Sherpa bags, the soft-sided mesh carrying cases developed by a former airline attendant and dog owner. Unlike crates, these bags can be easily grabbed and carried over your shoulder. So if your plane is going down, just seize the bag from under the seat on your way out.

NOTE: there's only the most remote chance you will ever need all this information, but perhaps it will help you stay calmer in an emergency to know that *both* of you can make it out safely!

Questions Most Often Asked
of "Dog Lawyers"

What are "dog lawyers?" They're people whose practice has gone to the dogs, like Linda Cawley of Denver, Colorado, who handles lawsuits concerning dogs. They are also lawyers who have written books about laws pertaining to dogs, like *Dog Law* by Mary Randolph and *Dogs and the Law* by Anmarie Barrie of LaVergne & Barrie, in Neptune, New Jersey.

Here are the types of questions these people are often asked and what they and others have written or said:

Can I leave money to my dog?

In the eyes of the law, a dog is not a person but personal property, and you can't leave money to property. But you can leave money to a person to take care of your dogs.

My dog was accidentally killed and it was entirely another person's fault. What kind of damages can I get if I sue?

This varies from state to state, but generally you can only get back the value of your dog. What's taken into account is the purchase price, the breed, whether she was pregnant, whether it was a show dog, etc. However, New York attorney Albert Podell points out that if the accident happened right next to you, and it was very gory, you may have grounds for an independent suit because you were personally impacted by the trauma.

Can I collect for the terrible pain and suffering I went through?

"Generally, you are not going to get large damages for pain and suffering, because the court views your dog as personal property, like a desk. If someone ruined your old roll-top desk, a court would only consider the value of that desk." (Barrie)

In a different situation, a woman once collected $700 for mental anguish when she opened the casket at her dog's funeral and found a dead cat inside. (Randolph)

Also, Linda Cawley once won a $24,000 recovery for the wrongful death of a chow who died of brain damage from heat prostration at the groomers because of their broken air conditioner.

Can someone sue me for the pain and suffering they claim my dog caused them?

"Yes. If your dog bit and injured somebody and they were hurt, they can sue you for millions, the same as if they slipped and fell outside your house. They may be able to prove that they needed medical treatments, medication, physical therapy, counseling (to get rid of their fear of dogs), and that they sustained a loss of earnings because they couldn't leave their house since their leg was so torn up." (Barrie)

In one case, a Los Angeles dog owner had to pay his neighbors $6,000 out of court because of his dog, which barked all day. Another time, a pet owner was ordered to pay *$2.6 million* after two people were thrown from the back of a truck when the vehicle they were riding in swerved to avoid an unleashed dog.

Are pooper scooper laws legally binding?

Yes. "An Orthodox Jew fought it in court once, saying he was forbidden from picking up litter on the Sabbath, and the law interfered with his free exercise of religion." He lost. (Randolph) Note: assistance dogs are often exempt from pooper scooper laws. (Barrie)

My little Motzie cost me a fortune in medical expenses this year. Can I deduct her as a dependent?

"You may think of your dog as a dependent member of the family, but the IRS doesn't. They once refused a woman who wanted 'head of household' rates because she lived with 25 dogs and cats. You may be able to deduct your dog if he or she is a guide or specially trained service dog." (Randolph)

My dog was "accidentally arrested," or wrongfully picked up by a shelter. Can I sue them?

"Probably not. "The law acknowledges only injury to you, not your dog. You may be able to collect some money for your mental distress, but not your dog's." (Randolph)

Since this is a free country, can I have as many dogs as I want?
"Usually you can in rural areas, but many cities restrict residents to two or three dogs per household, except for puppies. You may need a special permit, if you want more." (Barrie)

My husband and I are divorcing. What happens if we both want sole custody of our dog?
In one case, a divorcing couple was so hostile that they put the dog to sleep rather than allow one of them to care for it. (*Wall Street Journal*)
"A dog may be contested property in divorce proceedings. A court will determine custody and visitation rights." (Barrie)
"And don't forget to put in a claim for support and pup-keep." (Podell)

Can I get an insurance policy for my dog?
"Your homeowner's or renter's policy may already cover your dog, but you might need additional coverage. If your dog has bitten someone, however, you probably can't get it." (Barrie)
Attorney Albert Podell says many states have a "one-bite rule," which means that the dog's owner cannot be held liable in negligence to anyone bitten by the dog unless the dog had either previously bitten someone or clearly demonstrated a vicious propensity.

When my dog dies, can I bury him in my backyard?
"Although people do, many towns have ordinances against it. It's best to have your vet handle the burial." (Barrie)

I have a dog although it's against my lease. Can we be evicted?
"Yes, but if the clause has not been enforced for a long time, the landlord may have lost his right to object." (Barrie)

How You–and Your Children–
Can Avoid Being Bitten by a Dog

Two to three million dog bites are reported to local authorities each year—and millions more go unreported. Here is some advice from J. Michael Cornwell, D.V.M., who teaches courses in protection, and has also developed a children's video program called "Safety Is Fun."

Never rush past an attacking dog or turn your back and run away. The dog's natural inclination is to chase and catch something that runs from him.

Don't make fast, jerky movements. Especially toward an attacking dog's head or eyes.

Act unconcerned. Keep still and hold your ground, or walk slowly, saying something softly like "nice dog." Your seeming lack of concern may be all that is necessary.

Don't ever stare into a dog's eyes. It may anger him, because that's how dogs challenge each other to a fight.

If you're riding a bicycle, and can't outrace the dog past his territory, place your bike between you and him. At the same time, say "Go home," or something similar, and pretend to throw something at him.

Jump onto a car hood or even climb a tree. Better to be embarrassed then bitten.

If you're walking with a small child, don't lift him or her. A child's dangling legs make an easy target for the dog. It's better to stand between the dog and the child.

Speak softly, back away, and tell your child to stay directly behind you.

If all else fails and you're about to be bitten:

Feed him your jacket—or your purse or anything else that can come between you and the dog. If that fails, *lie still, face down on the ground.* Fold your fists (don't interlace your fingers), and put them

Are Dog Bites or Cat Bites More Dangerous?

According to James Miller, D.V.M., cats' mouths aren't necessarily dirtier than dogs', but cat *bites* have a tendency to become more infected. Dr. Miller says that between 30 and 50 percent of all cat bites become seriously infected, because cats have fine, needlelike teeth and they're almost injecting that bacteria under the skin. Dog bites have a tendency to be open and bleed more, which helps clean the wound out.

behind your neck while covering your ears with your forearms. Don't move because continued motion can send dogs into a frenzy of attack. Lying like this not only protects your face, but it's also a nonthreatening position to animals.

If it's a stray dog, memorize descriptive characteristics. You want to notice whatever you can about him so that if necessary, he can be found again for possible testing. Also, "observe where the dog goes after he leaves you," says Cornwell, who is the director/owner of the Glencoe Animal Hospital in Columbus, Ohio.

Children are most often the target of dog bites, and teaching them the above is good, but if they're very young, Dr. Cornwell has devised a better way for them. He counsels teaching young children that if they're about to be attacked they should *make believe they're a tree.* Trees don't move, so they should stand extremely still. If they are attacked, they should drop to the ground and *make believe they're a log.* Logs don't move—and dogs don't attack logs.

You might also want to teach your children how to avoid getting into a position where they're likely to be bitten in the first place. Most of the following will work for you, too.

1. Never go up to a strange dog, particularly one that's confined in a yard, or tied up to a fence, or a tree.
2. Never go into a house or a yard where there is a dog if the owner isn't there.
3. Never pet a dog without asking the owner's permission first.
4. Never pet a dog without letting it sniff you first. Teach children

Dogs Most and Least Likely to Bite

In a study on biting and nonbiting dogs, you may have expected German shepherds and chow chows to be among the biters. But collies? Yes, and even more surprising, the pit bull *didn't* bite. But, since there was only one pit bull in the study, it doesn't mean much.

The study, published in the June 1994 issue of the journal *Pediatrics*, reported that the dogs least likely to bite were golden retrievers, Chihuahuas, poodles, and Scottish terriers. This study, conducted in Denver, Colorado, for the Centers for Disease Control in Atlanta, also found that biters tended to be male and unneutered, and more likely to live in homes with children.

to curl their fingers into their palms and let the dog sniff the backs of their hands. The dog may also want to sniff other parts of their bodies. Explain to them that that's how dogs say hello and find out who someone is.

5. Never disturb a dog who is eating.

6. Never attempt to pick up or handle puppies when the mother is there.

7. Never walk up from behind a dog to pet it. The dog may be startled.

8. Stay away from an injured animal.

9. Don't tease a dog, or take a toy or a bone away from him.

10. Never reach into a car to pet a dog.

11. Never lunge at a dog.

What Your Dog Can Hear,
Smell, and See—and Can He Watch TV?

Dogs Can Hear a Heck of a Lot Better Than We Can

Dogs with erect or pricked ears hear better than flop-eared dogs, but all can hear higher ranges than we can, including sounds inaudible to us. This is helpful to them in the wild, because they can hear bats and rodents emitting high-pitched ultrasonic sounds. It supposedly helps them domestically, enabling them even to hear cockroaches or mice in the walls, although it's uncertain why they would want to.

One thing they probably can't hear in the walls, or the woods, though, is a ghost. When dogs are walking in the woods, and suddenly freeze when everything is completely silent, excitable owners have occasionally claimed afterward that their dogs must have seen a ghost. A more logical explanation, overlooked by many, is that the dog's hearing is so keen that he simply heard something that his owner could not hear.

Dogs can also *locate* sounds better than we can. While we're stuck with unattractive appendages that never move, dogs can flick their graceful ears in many directions to collect sounds, and then pinpoint their source.

Dog can also *distinguish* sounds better than we can. They can pick up the sounds of our footsteps when we're walking 50 yards away with traffic all around us, or recognize the sound of our car engine as opposed to the neighbor's.

Interesting experiment: dogs react to a hissing sound made through the teeth. Ssssso, ssssay "SSSSSsit" to your dog and you'll sssseee.

Can Dogs See in Mirrors?

Puppies may initially react to a reflection as though it were another animal, but as they mature, according to Cornell University's Dr. Katherine A. Haupt, they "habituate to the mirror image when they realize that
what they're looking at doesn't smell like a dog or bark like a dog. So
they ignore it." If they look in the mirror, "dogs don't seem to recognize
that it's themselves." When we asked why, she replied diplomatically,
"Some people feel they're not intelligent enough."

If you'd like to prove those people wrong, try to put something on
your dog's head without his realizing it, and set him in front of a mirror.
If you can do that, and he looks in the mirror, and then tries to swat off
the object, your dog is a genius.

Dogs Can Smell a Heck of a Lot Better Than We Can

Saying to someone "you ain't nothing but a hound dog" may not be
grammatical, but it's probably a compliment. Dr. Bruce Fogle writes
in *The Dog's Mind* that dogs have 220 million smell-sensitive cells in
their noses compared to 5 million in ours; they have more than ten
times more nasal membranes than we do—and we're bigger.

The result: some say dogs are one million times better at odor
detection than we are; some say ten million; others, 100 million times
better. It may depend on what they're smelling. They're not so good
at odors that have no significance to them, like flowers, but let them
smell emotions like fear or hate and they'll soon start nosing around.

This is especially true where sweat is concerned. Desmond Morris writes in *Dogwatching* of the time six men each picked up a pebble and threw it as far as they could. A dog was then allowed to sniff
the hand of each, after which it was no sweat for the dog to suc-
cessfully find and retrieve his pebble.

In one area, their scent-abilities are hard to believe. Bloodhounds
can track human feet even when shoes have been worn, and the trail
is four days old. Dogs are also tuned in to the smell of people's bodies in general. In one study, dogs could tell whether twins were iden-

tical or fraternal, since identical twins have the same body scent. In another commonly reported experiment, they could smell the difference between children who were autistic and those who were not.

Dogs Don't See As Well As We Do

They have more rods, which is probably why it was believed for years that they could only see in black and white. But now we know that they can also see some slight tints of color, like looking at a light pastel.

Studies at the University of California at Santa Barbara, and reported in a January 1990 *Scientific American* article entitled *See Spot See Blue*, reported that dogs can easily tell a red ball from a blue ball. They can also tell white from colored light, and can distinguish between closely related hues of violet and blue.

Like people with red-green color blindness, however, they can not discriminate colors from greenish yellow through orange to red. Seeing-eye dogs actually can't distinguish between red and green traffic lights. They're trained to watch the traffic patterns, so it doesn't matter. In fact, none of this matters to dogs; they aren't interested in color.

Dogs also have limited three-dimensional vision. Most have a wider field of vision than we have, especially narrow-headed dogs with eyes on the sides of their heads. Dogs can also see slight movement over a wide area extremely well, although they're not that good at detail. If someone stands perfectly still far away, your dog can barely see it. Try it. Remain motionless 300 yards away and your dog can't see you. Now you know why he sometimes ignores you when you're far away, and you won't be insulted.

Dogs Can See Television—a Little Bit

There's some disagreement about whether dogs can see television, but according to Katherine Haupt, V.M.D., Ph.D., editor of *Cornell University Animal Health Newsletter*, "There's no reason why dogs can't watch television."

Still, many dogs don't seem particularly interested in what's on the tube. They may *seem* to be watching, but look carefully and you'll

What Color Is Your Dog Food?

The color of dog food may be one reason dogs live longer and better lives today than they did a decade or so ago. "They used to put a lot of red dye in dog food even though dogs are color blind," says Robert Brown, D.V.M., owner of the Cherrydale Veterinary Clinic in Arlington, Virginia. "It was done to appeal to the purchaser, but there's no doubt it harmed the dogs." He also warns that the practice is being continued today by outlet or generic-type dog food producers, "if they think they can get away with it."

John Stossel on ABC News *20/20* explained that the coloring in dog food is put there for *us*, not for our dogs, because we buy what we think our pets will like—and we think they will like what we like.

So what color is our dog food really? If it wasn't colored, when it comes out of the can (which dog food manufacturers called the "plop factor"), he said we might see *black* food. Some of it by law has to be covered with charcoal to make sure no one sells it as people food.

note that they're probably just sitting happily next to you. *That's* what they're really interested in. Television time to them means you're sitting down, relaxing, and a lap is available.

One last interesting fact in the TV-or-not-TV question. Dogs can see television much better in England than in the United States. American television transmits at 525 lines per second, so our dogs just see a lot of fast moving dots. But in England, pictures are transmitted at 625 lines per second, which creates a clearer scene. This has led to all kinds of strange letters-to-the-editors in English magazines and newspapers, arguing over which shows dogs like better! Over here, *Frasier* and reruns of *Lassie* would probably easily win, paws down.

The Most Expensive Gifts
You Can Buy Your Dog

Do you want to put on the dog with some spectacular and outrageous items? Leigh Applebrook, co-owner of The Pet Department Store in New York, tells you about the first four:

1. A wedding. If you're a party animal who wants to marry off your dog, "We will provide the minister, rabbi, or priest; 1,000 yards of bridal veil, wedding rings made out of cigar bands, and a dogwood bridal bouquet for your dog to throw out to the other pooches. Also, a doggie wedding cake made out of venison and lamb for the happy couple, and a 3-foot-high wedding cake for their guests, made of low-sugar carrot cake so the people-guests can share their cake with their dogs." A 60-minute free video is made of the event for you, they guarantee media coverage, and you can invite 150 people and their dog guests for only $5,000.

2. Your very own Paw-casso. Your dog can be painted into a picture to match your apartment—or your yacht. The Pet Department Store arranges to have your dog painted in a costume for a particular period, "perhaps Madame Bovary, or a black-and-white painting of your dog on a Harley Davidson à la Marlon Brando in the fifties." Or, if you prefer, their artist "will paint in your favorite Bulgari jewelry on your dog, and he'll put cleavage on you if you don't have it," promises Leigh Applebrook, who, with her husband, Roger, owns the trendy Manhattan store, where Madonna buys leashes and collars, and they may be for more than her dog. Cost of the painting: $3,000 to $15,000.

3. Doggie treadmill. An actual treadmill that has an 11 percent incline. "They're made for us by the same company that makes assembly line conveyor belts for Ford trucks and UPS." They

How to Save Money on Dog Food

- Buying in bulk may *not* save you money. Purchasing more than your pet can consume in a month just leads to spoiled food, which has to be thrown away.

- Since wet foods consist of as much as 75 percent water, consider switching from moist to dry, which costs less, and supplies more nutrition pound for pound.

- Nan Weitzman and Ross Becker say that if you want to save money on dog food, *don't* buy cheap food. It costs less to use a super premium dog food than an economy dog food because of the nutritional power of the food, they report in their book, *The Dog Food Book*.

In one test they conducted for *Good Dog!*'s March-April food-testing issue, they had to feed five times as much of the economy brand dog food to get the same nutritional benefits of the super premium brand. In addition, a study reported in the newsletter *The Kennel Doctor* revealed that thirteen dogs suffered severe dermatitis from generic-type food. Note: generic food doesn't say "generic" on the label. Just watch out if it's too cheap, and be wary if it doesn't come from a pet outlet.

weigh 300 pounds, and cost $3,000 to $4,000. You can run on it along with your dog.

4. A year of weekly aerobic exercises with your dog. It's $100 for a 15-minute session of joint exercises and treadmill run with a trainer. You get a sweat suit for your dog, personalized with his name on it, and a video to take home so you can continue your exercise program.

If you do it weekly, they will give your dog a massage rub-down each week after the exercises: "Your cocker spaniel or Chihuahua sits on your feet and you lift your leg slowly one to three, down one to three," says Applebrook. Cost: $5,000 a year.

5. Beau Bradford, of Los Angeles, is a Degas of dogs, who will paint your dog into a well-known work of art. Wouldn't you want your

dog's face substituted for the Mona Lisa's or your dog painted right onto the lap of a Modigliani nude? Hugh Hefner did, and so have many others who could afford the $3,500 starting fee, with $500 more for each dog that's added to the painting. For more information, contact Beau Bradford, 8721 Santa Monica Blvd., #243, West Hollywood, California 90069.

6. Got any money left? At Le Chien in Manhattan, owner Lisa Gilford promises that they'll make you the same dog collar they made for Elizabeth Taylor's dog: a diamond and sapphire collar for, oh, a mere $4,000.

7. Or for $500 to $1,500, they'll make you a doggie necklace with a gold chain, a small heart and a tiny diamond.

8. For $3,500, they'll sell you a four-poster gold-leaf canopy bed, so you can let your sleeping dog lie there. This one was also good enough for Elizabeth Taylor, so it should be good enough for your dog.

Fear of Thunder and Scared
on the Fourth of July

The Fourth of July is no picnic for most pet owners! Nor are most thunderstorms, "which can turn your peaceful, quiet pooch into a Tasmanian devil dog," says William Fortney, D.V.M.

This assistant professor of clinical medicine at Kansas State University College of Veterinary Medicine in Manhattan, Kansas, says that helping your dog to handle these traumas could not only save his psyche, it could save his life. When dogs have heard the sounds of thunder, or the snap, crackle, or pop of fireworks—especially fireworks for the first time—they have jumped out of windows, leaped through screen or glass doors, or simply run away to hide, and never seen again.

Unfortunately, when these sounds begin, most loving dog owners do the exact opposite of what they should do. "When your frightened dog comes to you, and you let him get on your lap, or couch, or bed to sleep with you, you're reinforcing this fearful behavior and encouraging it in the future," says Fortney. He suggests you "instead distract him by playing fetch or some activity he enjoys, or give him a treat he really likes."

Another possibility is to divert his attention with other sounds. Professional trainer Kate Delano Condax writes in *101 Training Tips for Your Dog* that you should distract your dog by playing loud music with a strong percussion beat. Then the thunder will not sound as bad to your dog because it won't suddenly burst out from a quiet background.

Unfortunately that only masks the problem; it doesn't solve it. Many animal behaviorists suggest you desensitize your dog to these noises. You can start by taping the sound your dog is afraid of, or by buying a tape of these sounds, which is sold in some pet shops or by mail.

Mineral Oil May Help Dogs Overcome the Fear of Thunder

In a press release by Nature's Recipe, Alfred J. Plechner, D.V.M., suggested that people place a small amount of mineral oil in their dog's ear to lessen the pain and discomfort of thunder or fireworks noise.

Dr. Plechner, of Los Angeles, said the mineral oil will "coat the tympanic membrane of the inner ear and will muffle the intense vibrations associated with loud noises," according to S.A. Marcus's "Pets" column in *Newsday*.

Then, play this scary stimulus for him at a low level while petting and praising him at the same time.

Gradually increase the volume after a while, continuing the reinforcement throughout. Since this may take a month or so, if you're preparing your dog for the Fourth of July, start training in advance.

In addition to a tape recording, Fortney advises you to prepare your dog for the fireworks by "having someone with a cap gun fire it in another room. Praise your dog as the gun is fired. But don't let your dog see the person with the cap gun because then he may just become afraid of the gun."

Other suggestions of Fortney's are that if you take your dog for a walk right before an anticipated storm, or on the Fourth of July, keep him tightly on his leash. And if you think he will need tranquilizers, don't wait until the last moment to call the vet or you may not be able to get an appointment.

Jay Empel, D.V.M., advises people not to let their dogs wander around outdoors during the holiday. Dr. Empel expressed concern that they might run away—or that some youngster may toss a firecracker at them.

"Dogs could be burned, or suffer hearing or vision loss if firecrackers are set off too close to them," says the Atlanta veterinarian. "If you're the one setting off the fireworks, be sure to dispose of everything afterward, or your dog may swallow something and develop a serious injury," says this owner of Vernon Woods Animal Hospital.

How to Keep the Airlines
from Killing Your Dog

"We're sorry about the loss of your baggage," an airline representative wrote to a woman whose pet they had accidentally killed. Unfortunately, airlines do consider pets to be luggage, and considering how they treat that, no wonder people are frightened about flying with their dogs.

Statistics are hard to come by, but the *Los Angeles Times* found that in one recent year, seventy pets had died. Many deaths aren't reported, however, and many dogs don't die but are permanently injured or lost as a result of their trip.

That's what happened to Bud Brownhill of Anaheim, California, whose dog was left deafened and neurologically damaged after a flight. He's now the international chairman of Dog Owners for International Travel (DO-IT), and he and others offer ideas on keeping the airlines from killing or injuring your dog.

- Talk to a supervisor when you get to the airport and tell him you've got an extremely valuable dog in terms of dollars—even if it's a mutt. Otherwise, some baggage handlers couldn't care less if you were carrying a rock.

- When you board the plane, say to the pilot, "I've got this dog on the plane and it's worth a lot of money. Please make sure to turn on the heat and the pressurization." This is done from the cockpit, and someone may have forgotten to give the pilot that information. Cargo departments can get as hot as 140 degrees, and intense cold can be just as damaging.

- Put large strips of red or orange fluorescent material all over the crate so you can spot it halfway across the airport and your dog won't get mixed up with anything else.

277 Secrets Your Dog Wants You to Know

- Put arrows or the words "Top" and "Live Animal" on top of the crate to "make sure your dog doesn't fly upside down."

- Make certain your home addresses and phone numbers, plus those of where you're going, are large and attached in several places in case your dog bites one off. A few of the stickers should be outside the crate, because many people won't reach in a kennel for fear of being bitten.

- Watch the ticket clerk attach the destination tags at the airport. Make sure it says Detroit if that's where you're going.

- Get your dog used to hearing airplane noises by taking him for a drive on a busy highway. Otherwise, it's a horror story for an overprotected dog in a cold, unpressurized, noisy crate for the first time.

- Before your dog's first flight, get him used to sitting and eating in a crate. Put his food and some blankets in there, and don't put the top on. Next, put the top on but not the door. Then put the door on but don't close it.

- Sedating your dog is a lazy way of getting him used to the crate. Avoid it unless your vet recommends it.

Other interesting ideas people have suggested:

- Freeze a plastic margarine cup filled with water so it melts slowly during the trip in the crate to provide drinking water.

- Make sure your crate has sturdy handles that won't come off during rough baggage handling.

- Avoid flying at the busiest times, so the airport personnel will be able to give you and your dog more personal attention.

- If you must change planes, don't make the connections too close, so there's time for your pet to switch planes as well.

- Ask the airline if you can watch your dog being loaded and unloaded at the cargo hold.

- Keep your dog's nails clipped so they won't get caught in the crate's door.

- The Humane Society has issued a warning that pug-nosed breeds, like Pekingese, chow chows, Boston terriers, and English bulldogs, can suffocate in a cargo hold.

- Don't fly when it's too cold or too hot. Delays on the Tarmac can be fatal. Book an early morning flight in summer or a late evening flight in winter to avoid temperature extremes.

- If you don't have a small dog you can take along in the cabin with you and keep under the seat, consider leaving your dog at home.

Celebrities Who Have
Your Type of Dog

Here are some celebrities who own dogs—or is it the dogs who own the celebrities? These canines really live in the lap of luxury, and some of their owners go "dog-wild" over them. Elizabeth Taylor's largess is legendary. Betty White reportedly is leaving five million dollars to animals. And Richard Simmons has decorated his apartment in dalmatian spots to match his dogs.

We put together the following list by calling animal hospitals like the Brent-Air Animal Hospital in California, examining photographs of celebrities with their dogs in newspapers, and dog photo books, such as *Top Dog: Canines and Their Companions* by Walker, Haynsworth, and Levy, and *Name That Dog*, by Lynn Hamer. As best as we could tell, all these dogs are currently owned by these people. Previous dogs don't count, which is why we didn't mention things like Bill Clinton having owned a cocker spaniel before his cat named Socks.

American Bulldog	Sly Stallone
Basset Hound	Mary Tyler Moore
Beagle	Barry Manilow
Bernese Mountain Dog	Robert Redford
Bichon Frise	Betty White
Bordeaux Mastiff	Bob Dylan
Borzoi	Bo Derek
Boxer	Carroll O'Connor
	Sly Stallone
	Charlton Heston
Brussels Griffon	Mary Tyler Moore
Cairn Terrier	Liza Minnelli
Chihuahua	Paula Abdul
	Martina Navratilova

The Richest Dogs on Record

According to the *Guinness Book of Pet Records*, the richest dog in America was a poodle named Toby, who was left fifteen million dollars (worth perhaps fifty million today) by a woman who died in 1931. While the owner was alive, Toby slept on expensive silk linens, and ate breakfast in bed off silver trays brought by a special butler.

After the owner died, disputes arose about her will. While her relatives duked it out, Toby slept in a plain wooden basket in the kitchen, eating out of an ordinary bowl. Two years later, Toby was put to sleep by the executors of the will.

The richest dog in the world today stands to "inherit" between twelve and eighty million dollars (reports vary), and has a maid, chauffeur, limousine, and Jacuzzi. Most important, "Guenther IV" has a lawyer (his owner), which he needs, because he lives in Italy, the money left to him is in Germany, and there are international disputes contesting the bizarre will.

Chow Chow	Martha Stewart
	Sally Struthers
	Kelsey Grammer
Collie	Bo Derek
Dachshund	Dick Clark
	Mickey Rooney
Dalmatian	Connie Sellecca
	Gloria Estefan
	Richard Simmons
	John Tesh
Doberman	Raquel Welch
English Sheepdog	Walter Matthau
German Shepherd	Melissa Gilbert
	Stephanie Powers
	Charlton Heston
	Chuck Woollery
Great Dane	Kelsey Grammer
Greyhound	Bo Derek

The Most Popular AKC-Registered Breeds in America

Here is the list, according to the latest American Kennel Club figures.

- Labrador Retrievers
- Rottweilers
- Shepherds
- Cocker Spaniels
- Golden Retrievers
- Poodles
- Beagles
- Dachshunds
- Dalmatians
- Shetland Sheepdogs
- Pomeranians
- Yorkshire Terriers
- Shih Tzus

Irish Wolfhound	Sally Jessy Raphael
Jack Russell Terrier	Prince Charles
	Sarah Ferguson, the Duchess of York
Lhasa Apso	Phyllis Diller
Maltese	Brooke Shields
	Elizabeth Taylor
Mastiff	Kirstie Alley
	Marlon Brando
Mixed Breed	Ricki Lake
Norwich Terrier	Lily Tomlin
Pekingese	Betty White
Poodle	Jack Lemmon
	Ivana Trump
	Janine Turner
	Betty White

Poodle	Barbara Walters
Pug	Sally Jessy Raphael
Retrievers (Labrador Retrievers, Golden Labradors, and Golden Retrievers)	
	Kirstie Alley
	Dick Clark
	Phil Donahue
	Gordon Elliott
	Kirk Douglas
	Henry Kissinger
	Mary Tyler Moore
	Gregory Peck
	Geraldo Rivera
	Arnold Schwarzenegger
	James Stewart
	Betty White
	Oprah Winfrey
	Dan Quayle
Saint Bernard	Carl Reiner
	Betty White
Schnauzer	Bo Derek
	Arte Johnson
Sharpei	Geraldo Rivera
Shih Tzu	Zsa Zsa Gabor
Springer Spaniel	George and Barbara Bush
Weimaraner	Dick Clark
Welsh Corgi	Queen Elizabeth
Yorkshire Terrier	Joan Rivers

7 Strange Things Your Dog Could Be Allergic To—Plus 4 Common Allergies

If your healthy animal suddenly becomes a nose-dripper, an eye-waterer, a face-rubber, or a foot-licker, he may be allergic to something. But unlike people, who sneeze and have problems with their eyes and nose when they're allergic, dogs are more likely to scratch themselves.

"It's mostly their skin that bothers dogs," says Kansas State University veterinarian William Fortney. He says that if your dog is allergic, "you'll see him scratching, rubbing his face on the carpet or a hard spot, and sometimes he'll have ear infections, gastrointestinal upsets, and even a postnasal drip."

Dr. Fortney says allergies can be a serious problem for dogs because when they start scratching themselves, it can cause slow-to-cure skin conditions. Furthermore, says Dr. Fortney, "if a dog is itchy, he's probably miserable. People should take animal allergies seriously and seek relief immediately. Many dogs suffer needlessly because their owners don't believe they're really allergic—or they don't really care."

To start with, here are seven unusual things your dog could be allergic to, as outlined by Irwin Small, D.V.M.

1. **You.** (See page 76.)

2. **Their own clothes.** They may become allergic to those little sweaters or jackets that people put on them.

3. **Your clothes.** For example, your overcoat.

4. **Nicotine.** Allergies may be a potential problem, as well as cancer.

5. **Other animals.** Dog hairs or cat hairs.

6. **People food.** One dog became sick every time his owner slipped him his oysters. Dr. Small says many dogs also can't handle peaches, and get gastrointestinal symptoms.

Wear White Socks to Find Out If Your Dog Has Fleas

If your dog has fleas, chances are your house is infested with them, too. One way to tell if you've got a problem is to walk through your house with white socks on, according to Jeff Hahn, a University of Minnesota entomologist. If there are small black specks on your socks afterward, there are fleas.

Herbert Salm, D.V.M., has an interesting way for people to tell whether or not the little tiny black specks they may see around the house or on their pillows, are really fleas. Dr. Salm says to pick up these pepperlike pieces, put them on a white piece of paper or white napkin and put a little water on them. If the specks turn red, they're flea droppings, filled with blood.

Finally, Dr. William Fortney says that if you suspect fleas are on your dog, and you have tiny bites on you below the knees, your dog probably does have them. Fleas prefer that area, much like they prefer the rump end of the dog.

---

7. **Cosmetics and perfumes.** Dr. Small told of one case in which the dog had a such a severe reaction to his owner's perfume that he had to be hospitalized. "When his owner came to see him, she sat in a waiting room 30 feet away through closed doors and the dog still broke out," says the doctor, who is an associate dean and professor emeritus at the College of Medicine at the University of Illinois, and former president of the American Academy of Veterinary Dermatology.

Here are four common allergens, according to Dr. Fortney, and what you can do about them:

1. **Flea allergy dermatitis.** The fleas' saliva initiates the actual allergic reaction.

   How to tell if it's fleas: During warm weather, your dog will most likely be biting himself toward his tail. You may not see the fleas on him, however, for there can be a delayed reaction of 48 to 72 hours from the time the flea was on your dog until he starts biting.

What to do: Get rid of the fleas on his body *and* in your environment.

2. **Dog food.** He may be allergic to an ingredient in his diet, like beef, soy, beet pulp, dairy products, eggs, artificial colorings, food flavorings, or preservatives.

   How to tell: It's sometimes difficult, for a dog can develop an allergy to a food he's been eating right along. Blood tests are used, but the only way to confirm the diagnosis is to get rid of almost all the ingredients your dog is eating, and feed him something with just a few items in it as a test.

   What to do: Substitution is the easiest; try switching foods. If you're feeding soy-based food, try chicken, and so forth. Unfortunately, if the dog is allergic to a particular *ingredient,* it may be in the other food as well. Therefore, you can also switch the type of food, say from a cheaper food to a premium one. Don't change all at once, but mix in a little of the different food with his regular diet in increasing proportions. You may have to do a lot of experimenting, so keep a record of how much your dog scratches and other symptoms.

3. **Atopic or inhalation allergies.** Similar to people who have hay fever, dogs can be allergic to certain pollens, molds, and dust, and some of the odder items mentioned earlier.

   How to tell: They generally don't itch as severely as with other allergies. Instead of frantically licking and chewing their feet, they may scratch their armpits, have some redness of the ears, or rub their itchy faces along the carpet or on the furniture. Also, note when and where they're scratching. The ragweed season is July until the first frost. A spring allergy may be to trees. Spring and fall allergies can also be to mold and mildew because that's when it's in the house. Dust mites can be all year long, even in a clean house, but is more likely to be a problem when the house is dusty.

   What to do: Try to limit your dog's exposure to the allergen. If it's dust, use synthetic materials for his bedding. Water beds are

Fascinating Facts about Fleas

- It's been postulated that the rise in popularity of small lap dogs may have occurred because of fleas. Before the advent of pesticides, fleas were such a terrible problem that women may have chosen small dogs to distract them. When holding the small dogs to their chests or on their laps, they discovered some fleas went for the dog instead of them.

- There are said to be three thousand known species of fleas. Cat and dog fleas are closely related, but separate species. Surprisingly, cat fleas may be found on dogs.

the most dust-free. Keep humidity levels below 60 percent so mites can't reproduce. Get your dog out of the room before you dust or vacuum.

4. **Allergic contact dermatitis.** This can come from a flea collar, dyes in the carpet, his soap, shampoo, or a few items mentioned under strange allergies.

How to tell: Your dog's reaction will show up on the area in contact with the allergen. For example, his neck may break out if he's allergic to the insecticide in his flea collar. Or the parts of his body that touch his bed may become crusty if he's allergic to the materials in his bed.

What to do: Try substitution. If he's allergic to his steel collar, change to nylon or leather, or vice versa. Or stop using those items altogether. Be patient because these allergies can take a long time, sometimes months, to heal.

How to Teach Your Dog to
Do a Simple Card Trick

A poodle once performed an "amazing psychic" card trick on David Letterman's television show. After the dog's owner shuffled a deck of cards, she asked David to choose one card and show it to the audience. The cards were then reshuffled and the owner placed the deck on the floor. The dog, using "telepathic powers," found the card that Letterman had selected.

It isn't easy to teach an old dog this trick, but a young intelligent dog should be able to perform it. Furthermore, you can also add all kinds of dramatic flourishes so people think your pet is a genius—which we know he is.

To get your dog to do a trick, you can borrow a page from Hollywood history. When stars wanted a dog to lick them on the cheek, they put a little liverwurst *in* their cheeks. To do a card trick, put a tiny scraping of something like that under your fingernail. This is an old gambler's trick called a "daub," only instead of invisibly marking a card so your dog can *see* it, you're taking advantage of his superior olfactory sense so he can *smell* it.

Dennis Marks, a Hollywood writer/producer and creator of magic effects, tells how to go about doing a trick. Have someone select a card from any deck and hand the card back to you. Then, transfer a tiny amount of the hidden liverwurst from under your nail onto the face of the card so no one can see it. Put the liverwurst card on the bottom of the deck so it doesn't touch any other card, and make sure your liverwurst finger doesn't touch the other cards as well.

If you can do an overhand shuffle and keep that card on the bottom of the deck, do it. If not, just turn the deck with the faces toward you. Spread the cards between your two hands, always keeping the liverwurst card on the bottom. All this is easier than it may sound.

Bet Your Dog Can't Do This!

- Dogs on David Letterman's television show have twirled batons and "gone shopping."
- There's a dog who can hang glide.
- Television reporter Denise Richardson found a dog whose owner had taught him to play football—and another dog who scuba dives.
- *A Current Affair* featured a dog in Tallahassee, Florida, who could play the piano (almost).
- Reporter Diane Albright didn't *find* a dog who did a trick; hers accidentally drove her car.
- There's a dog in Flint, Michigan, who bowls.
- A dog in New York City goes skateboarding.
- In Hollywood, there was a Hungarian puli who fainted on cue and a Doberman who opened the car door.
- A woman in Maine says that her dog brought her the telephone with his mouth when she collapsed.
- A woman's dog in England did better. *Dogs Today* reported that a dog knocked the phone off the handset and his cries brought the police to the home. When they found blood on the handset, they assumed a violent crime had been committed. It turned out the puppy was teething.

Your next step is to look through the deck carefully as if you were searching for the card. Look back and forth at your dog and make a big deal out of it, as if you were getting signals from him. Then, slowly pull out the five or six cards from the deck, one at a time, with the backs of the cards to the audience. Make sure to include the liverwurst card.

Place these cards one foot apart in a line face down on the floor, the liverwurst card somewhere in the middle. Tell your dog to go find the card. Because of the liverwurst, he'll go to it—and everyone will be amazed.

How Dogs Track Drugs, People–and Termites

Ever wonder how the nose of a tracking dog knows what to look for? To train them to sniff out drugs, "You find out what the dog's toy drive is, whether they like to go after little plastic balls or a tug toy," says Correctional Sergeant Jeff Ashley, of the Indiana Department of Corrections. "Then, you hide their favorite toy with marijuana. Their main drive is to find that *toy* to play with, and later you can take the toy away." Since they associated the scent of the marijuana with the scent of the toy, they become trained to look for the drug.

Interestingly, he says expensive guard-type dogs are no longer being purchased by the DEA for this job. Ashley revealed that "they're now going to animal shelters rather than paying a lot of money for dogs. They're using dogs like small poodles, because people are leery if they see a big dog at the airport. But if they see a little poodle, everyone will think 'nice doggie' and not do a thing about it until they're busted with the drugs."

We visited Rikers Island Correctional Facility in New York City to see their K-9 corps. There, Captain Kathleen Ladalia, not only trains "green" dogs to hunt for marijuana, but also heroin, cocaine, hashish, and their derivatives. She also teaches dogs to scent guns by sniffing the oils they're cleaned with, as well as the gun powder itself.

Once trained, one job these dogs perform is to search visitors to Rikers Island. Right before the bus arrives, an announcement is made that anyone carrying drugs will be arrested—but that they can leave their drugs on their bus seat with no questions asked. Then the people are made to get out of the bus and line up. The dog zigzags through the empty seats, looking for—and often finding—drugs the visitors were planning to slip to the inmates.

If the people hide the drugs on or in their own bodies, "the dogs are trained not to jump on the person, but rather to sit down by

The Secret of Training Your Dog

If you believe hitting a dog works, think about what Mordecai Siegal and Matthew Margolis wrote in their best-seller, *Good Dog, Bad Dog:* "Imagine entering a taxi in a foreign country. The driver asks, 'Where to?' in his native tongue. You stare at him and shrug, not knowing the language. He then goes berserk and smacks you hard on the snout...."

Since that obviously isn't going to accomplish anything, what does work? Mordecai Siegal told us, "To merely *tell* your dog to do something means nothing. He must be *taught* how to sit, stay, heel, and learn to associate the utterance of specific words with the action of the commands they represent....

"Each action must be reinforced with rewards in the form of praise or compliments, thus conditioning him to do as you command out of an uncontrollable desire to obey. It's called motivating the dog. If it sounds like mind bending, that's exactly what it is," he adds. "It's also referred to as behavior modification."

---

their feet. If we see that, we have probable cause to believe they're carrying drugs, and they can be searched," says the trainer.

Jeff Ashley now trains dogs to track people rather than drugs. "One person plays the bad guy or the escapee and he lays the trail. The other one handles the dog and follows the trail. We take turns. I'll have my dog smell something like a T-shirt so he can scent on it. Then the other guy, another handler or a volunteer, will go out and lay the track." The dog will then follow the scent.

Dogs are even used in some places to scent out things like termites. These insects communicate with each other through pheromones, and when they digest their food, they give off methane gas. A dog can be trained to detect these odors through the permeable building materials.

How to Give Your Dog Pills, Liquid or Eye Medication, and Brush Your Canine's Canines

"Give him this three or four times a day," can be awful words to hear from your veterinarian. To make those pill-popping sessions less torturous for both of you, here are a few things you can do before you even start medicating him, according to Diane Arkins, writing in *Dog Fancy*.

- Store the pills or capsules in a closed container filled with moist, meaty treats. The medicinal smell will be reduced, and the pills will absorb a flavor the dog likes.

- Apply medical treatments in the bathroom or a small room so you don't have to chase your dog all over the house if he bolts. If you have a small dog, try wrapping him in a towel.

- Have everything ready in advance, so you don't have to set things up while you're holding him down.

- Catch him off guard emotionally. Enthusiastically announce something like: "Pills and treats." And, of course, always give him a treat, verbal or otherwise, afterwards.

- Always check the label to see if refrigeration is required with any medicine.

Giving pills: Now for the hard part. Most vets suggest that you wrap the pill (except for certain antibiotics) inside a soft food your dog likes, like cheese or small Vienna liver sausages. Of course, a sneaky dog might take the treat, thank you, and then spit the pill out, long after you think he's swallowed it.

It helps to wet capsules with water, or coat them with a little butter, margarine, or vegetable oil to make them go down better.

(Check with your vet first, because this shouldn't be done on all capsules.) Also, don't do this with pills, because if they start to dissolve before you get them in your dog's mouth, it could make them taste even worse.

As for actually getting the pills down, Herbert Salm, D.V.M., from Greenwich, Connecticut, says: "Tilt your dog's head back at a 45-degree angle. With one hand, hold the pill, and with the other, lower your pet's bottom jaw. Place the pill or capsule as far back in his mouth as you can, and then quickly remove your hand from his mouth. Immediately, put your dog's head back in a level position, and then either gently blow air into his nose region, or softly stroke his throat downward until you're sure he has swallowed the pill. If he licks his nose, he has."

Giving liquid medication: Arkins suggests that if you use a spoon, get a long-handled one, preferably larger than the amount of liquid you put into it, so it's more difficult for the liquid to spill out. Others have suggested you use a turkey baster; just don't use a glass one. Remember also to dress appropriately so you don't ruin an evening dress with splashed-on doggie medication.

As for administering the medicine, Dr. Salm recommends, "The best place to slip in the medicine is where the upper and lower lip come together at the corner. Hold your dog's head up, lift his skin there and slip the liquid right in. It will filter in and the dog will reflexively swallow it. Do it slowly so he doesn't inhale it. Also, don't hold his jaws shut tightly afterwards or he won't be able to swallow."

Finally, a licensed veterinary technician at an emergency veterinary hospital in Michigan wrote a letter to the editor of *Dog Fancy* stating that she had seen pets harmed by people who tried to toss pills to their dogs, or sneak up on them to give them their medication. This can "cause a pet to accidentally inhale its medication, which can cause obstruction, aspiration, pneumonia, or severe irritation to the lungs," she wrote. One *more* thing to worry about when you're trying to give your dog his medicine several times a day!

Applying eye medication: To apply liquid, Dr. Salm suggests you tilt your dog's head at a 45-degree angle. Put one hand on top of his head and apply the liquid with the other hand. If you're using

Are Rawhide Chews Effective—and Safe?

A study on rawhide bones, done at Harvard, and reported in *Pet Veterinarian*, found that rawhide strips *were* effective in removing dental calculus. But are they safe for your dog?

It depends on what they chew and where you buy them. As for the first, throw away the small pieces rather than letting your dog chew down to the last few inches. Small pieces can get stuck in their throats.

You also have to be careful where you buy them. Rawhide bones can be purchased inexpensively at flea markets, in those 99-cent-type places, and other suspect outlets. But rawhide from some parts of the world have traces of arsenic in them that comes from curing the raw cattle hides.

In the early 1980s, some dogs died after ingesting these rawhides, according to Doctors Foster & Smith's *Canine News*. Dangers still exist. The two vets claim cheap rawhides may be contaminated with insect eggs, or come from the hides of water buffalo which have a lot of fat, or may even have been washed with water that has high levels of mercury. So only buy genuine 100 percent rawhide bones from a respectable pet supply retailer.

a dropper, hold up his upper eyelid, and put the medication inside the top of the eye. Close his eyelids together and rub gently.

If you're using eye ointment, Dr. Salm advises that with clean hands, you apply a small amount to one finger. Then, pull down your dog's lower eyelid slightly, put a dab right inside the rim, close his eyes together, and rub gently. Using your finger will prevent the tube from poking him in the eye, and makes applying it much easier. Be careful also not to let the applicator touch your dog's eye, which can contaminate the medicine.

Cleaning the teeth: When he's a puppy, spend a few seconds at a time touching his lips and teeth to get him used to it. An article in *Veterinary Medicine* suggested you start by rubbing the teeth with cheesecloth dipped in bouillon to get the dog accustomed to dental care.

Then, start with a soft toothbrush and lots of praise. If you do this early in his life, you may avoid problems later. But since almost no one does, periodontal disease usually sets in, and by age five, most dogs have severe gum disease. Then you're punished for your earlier neglect by having to brush his teeth every day for the rest of his life—about as much fun as giving him medicine four times a day.

There are a number of commercial toothbrushes you can use, or a piece of gauze or nylon stocking that's been dipped in water (perhaps with a little garlic salt in it) and toothpaste works. Don't use your own foaming toothpaste; your dog could gag on it. Buy a special one for dogs.

Grasp your dog's jaw with your finger and thumb behind the long upper teeth (the space behind the canines). Gently pull his head up and back and his mouth will open. Brush his gums and teeth vigorously on both sides, from the gum line to the top of the tooth, in a circular motion. It's also important to brush the outside or cheek surface of the tooth where your dog's tongue can't easily reach, along with the back molars, which accumulate a lot of tartar. Do that every day.

Or try to.

How to Find Your Missing Dog and How to Keep from Being Scammed

We placed an ad in a local newspaper to look for people whose pets had been stolen. An alarming number of people who responded turned out to have been approached by con artists, after first being victimized by the tragedy of petnapping. Here's what we learned from these people, and especially from Sally Fekety, spokesperson for companion animals at the Humane Society of the United States, in Washington, D.C.

Are there any unusual ways that dogs are stolen these days?

Many petnappers are cruising neighborhoods with female dogs in heat. Soon, all the male dogs gather around.

Is there any way to increase your dog's chances of finding his way home if he's lost?

Put something you've recently worn in your yard, like the shirt you were wearing when he disappeared. (Cat owners have had success putting out their cat's litterbox.)

What are the most common ways in which dogs disappear or are stolen?

When they're left in a car, or outdoors, or tied up outside a store, or in the back of a pickup truck stopped at a light, or running free at a park. Even when they're behind a gate at home, they may dig a hole and get out, jump the fence, unhook or break a chain, unlock a gate, or escape when someone opens it.

What happens when they're taken?

It shouldn't happen to a dog. Stolen dogs are sold or used for research, breeding, guard dog training, animal sacrifice, food, and dog fighting. Large dogs are generally preferred for these purposes, but even a tiny pedigree bred dog (or cat) may be taken to teach dogs aggression.

Does tattooing dogs help?

Some researchers won't take an animal that has a tattoo or microchip, and will sometimes try to trace the owner. Don't put the tattoo on an ear; petnappers have cut them off.

What's the best time to search for a missing dog?

Some dogs hide during the day. Go out daily at dusk or dawn, when he may be out looking for food or a safer place.

Should you offer a reward and how much?

Yes, and larger ones work better. If someone has taken your dog for monetary purposes, if they can get more money from you, they may return him. Also, someone who finds him may keep him because he believes the dog isn't wanted because he is unleashed or has no collar. A large reward may convince him otherwise.

How can you be scammed for money if you don't offer a reward?

Commonly, someone calls the victim claiming to be an out-of-town trucker who drove through the area, found the dog on the highway, and now needs money to send him back and/or pay for his veterinary bills. Or someone will ask for an airline ticket so he can send your dog back, and then cash in the ticket.

How can someone who doesn't have your dog convince you that he does?

He'll call and say something like, "Does your missing dog have a black spot on its left ear and like to ride in cars?" And you may say, "No, my dog has a brown spot on its right ear and hates cars." Later, his confederate calls, saying he has a dog with a brown spot on its right ear who hates cars. You think he has your dog and send him the money he wants.

How can you tell if the person calling you really has your dog?

First, try asking him something that's *wrong*, like, "Does the dog you found have a black spot on its tail?" when your dog doesn't. Second, always hold back some small identifying characteristic in your ad or poster so you can see if the person calling you knows it and really does have your dog. Finally, if someone claims he needs money to pay a vet who treated your dog, call the vet. Even if he or she exists, the vet may not know anything about this.

Scary New Way to Steal Your Dog

Trainer Kate Condax writes in *101 Training Tips for Your Dog*, that in big cities, people with small dogs are being approached by friendly strangers who start patting their little pets. Suddenly, these monsters unsnap the dog's leash, throw the dog into a shoulder bag, jump into a car, and drive off with their dog.

Afterwards, there's usually a ransom demand, although some of these dogs may be sold to people who will throw them to the wolves—more likely the pit bulls—for dog fight training.

How should you arrange to meet with someone who claims to have your dog?

In a public place, since you'll be carrying cash.

Is there anything you can do that will increase your chances of finding your dog?

Keep up-to-date photos of him. Make a list of his colorings and the location of all his unusual markings. Always keep his collar on. Make sure the area he's kept in is secure, that no outsider could accidentally release him, that his collar isn't too loose (you should be able to slip two fingers between the collar and his neck), and that his collar and leash are right for his size and strength. When you're outside with him, keep him on his leash. Also, use a real identification tag; dogs can't be traced from rabies tags.

Do those nationwide registries of lost dogs work?

The problem is that most of them *mail* notices out to shelters, which may arrive too late at a shelter, which disposes of dogs in 48 to 72 hours. You can probably get to your dog faster than they can. Also, your dog may have a major injury and need expensive medical help immediately, which the shelter can't afford.

Whom should you call or contact if you're looking for your dog?

"Slap up *hundreds* of fliers at eye level and put them up within a ten-block area, not just a few posters on your block. Look and call everywhere and everyone. Alert the police, neighbors, shopkeepers,

How to Have Your Dog Tattooed

AKC Gazette suggests the following if you're going to tattoo your dog:

1. Don't tattoo large breeds until they're at least four months old, or small dogs until they're six to eight weeks, because the tattoo can become distorted when the dog gets larger. Most dogs don't need to be tranquilized for the procedure.

2. The recommended place is in the inside of the right thigh, and the area should be kept shaved and free of fur for visibility. Even so, tattoos are occasionally missed on heavy-coated breeds whose hair can hide the numbers.

3. There is no one central registering body for tattooed dogs in the United States. If your dog is AKC registered, they suggest you use those numbers and add "AKC" afterwards, because they will contact the owner of a missing dog if the finder calls them.

4. If your dog isn't AKC registered, several sources suggest you consider The National Dog Registry, Box 116, Woodstock, NY 12498, (800) 637-3647. They've been in business for twenty-five years, so unlike some of the entrepreneurial companies sprouting up, this one is likely to stick around.

5. Implanted microchips are promising, but someone who finds a dog with one has no way of knowing it, and the vet or shelter who gets him may not have a scanner—or use it.

UPS delivery men, construction workers, and limo drivers," says Florence Phillips, head of PetWatch in New York. Also, talk to people walking with dogs because they'll be the most concerned. Call local shelters and "pet" places within a 100-mile radius of your home, listed in your phone book under Humane Society, ASPCA, shelters, animal control, and veterinarians.

Any other suggestions?

Call local schools and see if you can get them to say something on the public address system. Children run around the neighborhood and may spot your dog.

Can you do anything now before your dog disappears?

Phillips says to make up color photos of your dog, and have extra copies on hand in case you ever need to give them out quickly to shelters and local vets.

Finally, if your dog disappears, it's important not to be so desperate that you do something foolish. As Sally Fekety says, "When you lose your dog, your brain isn't on right, and it's easy for people to take advantage of you in several different ways. You don't hear about some of these crimes because people are hesitant to say afterwards, 'I was an idiot and gave a stranger three hundred dollars.' Never give anybody any money until you see your dog."

Your Dog May Live Longer
Than Ever Before–and What He'll Die
of May Not Be What You Think

It has been said that the only fault of dogs is that their lives are too short. Indeed, most dogs die around ages eleven to thirteen, although *Natural Pet* magazine reports that two Austrailian dogs lived twenty-nine years and a Labrador retriever and a collie survived for twenty-seven years.

Sadly, that probably won't be true for your dog. Even so, there's a good chance he'll live longer than he would have a couple of decades ago, and most likely far longer than fifty years ago. "The average dog lives about twelve years now, and it was about seven in the nineteen thirties," says Guy Hodge, director of data and information for the Humane Society of the United States.

He explained: "Dogs and cats were utilitarian creatures, cared for only to the extent that they were useful. They weren't taken to veterinarians, there were no diagnostic tests, or programs for cure or prevention. There was no neutering, which tends to extend the animal's life expectancy by protecting the female dog from certain types of cancers, and reducing the male dog's inclination to roam, when he can get lost or hit by a car.

"Dogs slept outside," he continued. "They weren't bathed. There was no good-quality pet food—they were fed the scraps, and sometimes choked on bones."

Dr. Robert Brown, owner of the Cherrydale Veterinary Clinic in Arlington, Virginia, which specializes in canine geriatrics, agreed that improved food has played an important role in the increased longevity of canines. "Most of the money used to be put into advertising," he says, "and they put out a cheaper product. Today's food causes fewer difficulties, like stomach problems and diabetes."

In his opinion, flea control is also a factor, including the rise of "pyrethrin and permethrin sprays. They used to get rid of fleas by

When Does Your Dog Become Old?

Larger dogs have shorter life spans than small dogs. The American Animal Hospital Association in Denver put together this table to give an age-range for "old," which is based on a dog's size:

SMALL	20 pounds	9 to 13 years
MEDIUM	20 to 50 pounds	8 1/2 to 11 1/2 years
LARGE	51 to 90 pounds	7 1/2 to 10 1/2 years
GIANT	Over 90 pounds	6 to 8 1/2 years

The standard age table used to determine how old your dog is in human years is as follows:

When a dog is 3 months old, he's 5 "people" years; 6 months = 10 years; 1 year = 15 years; 2 years = 24; 3 years = 28; 4 years = 32; 5 years = 36; 6 years = 40; 7 years = 44; 8 years = 48; 9 years = 52; 10 years = 56; 12 years = 64; 14 years = 72; 16 years = 81; 18 years = 91; 20 years = 101 years.

putting strong compounds on animals, like DDT. Before that, they might take a hunting dog by the scruff of the neck and dip him in a strong insecticide—or even a motor oil."

Despite this hopeful picture, your dog is still likely to fall prey to certain illnesses that will ultimately kill him. But they might not be the diseases you'd think. There was an interesting study done a few years ago by the Denver-based Morris Animal Foundation, which funds studies of diseases in dogs and other animals.

They surveyed owners of more than two thousand dogs, asking what their leading health concerns were. Although cancer is actually the number-one cause of canine death, it was listed *third* among pet owners' concerns. People were more worried about obesity and nutrition, hip dysplasia, heart problems, bloat, arthritis, and kidney disease. In an earlier study, internal parasites were also a big fear of people, according to the *Advocate,* published by the American Humane Association in Colorado.

While some of those are certainly a contributing factor to dogs' deaths, the actual causes of death in elderly dogs, according to the

The Average Age of Dogs in America

According to the AVMA's Center for Information Management:

- 18 percent of American dogs are 1 year old or less.
- Almost 40 percent are 2 to 5 years old.
- 28 percent of the dog population is 6 to 10 years.
- Almost 14 percent are 11 years or older.

American Veterinary Medical Association, in Schaumburg, Illinois, is, first of all, accidents—which wasn't even mentioned as a factor dog owners worried about. Then came cancer, heart failure, and kidney disease (in that order).

A veterinarian in Irvine, California, Dr. Gayle Roberts told us that if you want to help your dog live longer:

1. Try to avoid accidents.
2. Keep his weight down. Obesity can hurt his joints, and lead to heart, kidney, skin, and digestive problems.
3. Since older pets become inactive and sleep most of the day, exercising an elderly dog is important for them, even if you only take them on short distances and walk slowly.
4. Keep teeth and gums healthy and clean. Gum disease can cause teeth to fall out, and the bacteria that caused the infection can weaken their immune system.
5. Spay or neuter a nonbreeding pet.
6. Limit stress. Older dogs don't like changes.

Dr. Roberts, who owns the Northwood Animal Hospital, added: "Today, hearing aids are being developed to correct deafness, cataract surgery to restore sight, there's hip replacement, chemotherapy and radiation treatment, cardiac ultrasound, ECG, [and] MRI for dogs and more. In the next decade dogs will live even longer."

How to Use Your Dog's Hair
to Make a Sweater

Several women throughout the world are giving a whole new meaning to the term "dog sweater." For them it may mean sweaters woven from the hairs of dogs. An entire book, *Knitting with Dog Hair*, has been written on the subject, and the co-author, Kendall Crolius, is getting used to people's surprised reactions. And she's also getting a bit tired of people asking her what would happen if she was wearing a dog sweater and walked by a fire hydrant!

Says Ms. Crolius enthusiastically, "Dog hair is a great way of making clothing from animals without killing them." Of course, one can also do this with wool from sheep; however, most people don't have many sheep around.

But those who live with dogs do have access to dog hair. All over their house with some breeds. Ms. Crolius and co-author Ann Montgomery write that "dog's hair is like mohair, angora, alpaca, or camel hair, only warmer." Crolius points out that another bonus of using it for knitting is that it's the ultimate in recycling: "You're making something out of what you used to throw away." If you're squeamish about wearing your dog, you can also use his yarn to, say, make a needlepoint picture not only of him, but *from* him.

Obviously some breeds are better than others for this, and Malise McGuire, a dog spinner in England, wrote us that she's had "various very nasty experiences with Old English sheepdog wool." Crolius has not. She also said she's done well with big shedding dogs, like Newfoundlands, Great Pyrenees, Hungarian pulis, or Samoyeds, which make fluffy fibers.

She counsels that one should use a stainless steel comb and a slicker brush to collect the long fibers of your dog. Then, sort through it and discard foreign matter. Use a good dog shampoo or laundry detergent and rinse and dry the fuzz gently. Wrap it in a towel

Go Ahead and Vacuum Your Dog

A vacuum cleaner keeps your pet's fur and skin free of dry skin flakes, flea dander, and fleas, according to Andrea Looney, D.V.M., as quoted in the newsletter *Bottom Line*.

Dr. Looney suggests using the upholstery brush attachment for about ten minutes on short-haired dogs and twice as long for long-coated ones. Keep the vacuum moving and avoid direct suction. Skip the tail.

If your dog is skittish because of the sound, Dr. Looney, an instructor at New York State College of Veterinary Medicine in Ithaca, says to get him used to the vacuum cleaner noise by turning it on for a while before you turn it on him.

overnight and let it dry fully. Keep the collected fur packed loosely in a sealed brown paper grocery bag and store it in a cool dark place, not a garage or basement.

If you'd really like to get into this, her book has a lot of information, patterns, and names of people who will knit for you if you don't know how. Go ahead: be the first in your dog club with a *real* Shih Tzu sweater or Lhasa apso leg warmers. (Mikhail Baryshnikov reportedly wears leg warmers made from his dogs.)

To find spinners, Connie Rudd, an Oregon spinner, tells people to contact the textile department at a local college, or the Handweavers Guild of America Inc., 2402 University Ave., Ste. 702, Minneapolis, MN 55114.

An amusing note to this whole phenomenon was penned by Tom Ferrell at the *New York Times Book Review*. After jocularly stating that dogs were "scandalously underutilized," he wrote that "they do not go to the office and lick envelopes; they do not pull their own weight, except in Alaska.... [They] do [not]...spin. But they can *be spun*."

6 Reasons People Look Like Their Dogs

1. People may choose a dog in the first place that looks like them, because they buy what they admire—and they like the way they look. So thin people may choose Afghans, and pudgy people might pick bulldogs.

2. They buy a dog that has the same characteristics so they're comfortable with the dog. For example, a short woman might choose a tiny dog; a large man might select a Hungarian vizsla.

3. They buy a dog they can handle, which is why you rarely see small people walking big dogs.

4. They take care of the dogs in the same way they care for themselves. A woman who doesn't have the time or the inclination to comb her own hair carefully may have an ungroomed dog with knotted hair.

5. They buy a dog that says for them what they're trying to say about themselves. For example, that they're small and shy (maybe a papillon), or that they're tough and macho (a pit bull).

6. They have their dog groomed to look like themselves because they like that style. For example, those who like short curly hair may want that for themselves and for their poodle. Or a man who shaves his head may buy a hairless dog.

But grooming a dog like one's self isn't always unintentional. Vinnie Constantino, head groomer at Le Chien in New York, says, "Many people come in saying 'I want my dog to look like me.'" Usually they comply, although they were a bit dismayed by the woman with a spiked Mohawk who insisted they groom her Yorkie the same way!

The 6 Best Dogs
to Guard Your Home

While all dogs may be created equal, not all are equally created as guard dogs. Certain dogs are better suited for taking a bite out of crime by going after the criminals. What kind should you get? One of the most famous guard dog trainers, Captain Haggerty, says, "If you're not guarding the U.S. Mint at Fort Knox, and you just don't want someone entering your home, the following dogs will do that well.

"German shepherds: If you want to go overboard, guard your home with an alligator and a moat around your house and an unstable dog in it. But if you have people coming over, especially kids, you want something realistic and controllable like a German shepherd. "This is the best all-around guard dog. They don't get overly aggressive and they don't go crazy.

"Pit bulls are good watch dogs; it's their owners who are sometimes bad. One recent study showed that pit bulls who killed had a higher percentage of owners with criminal backgrounds.

"Despite their negative publicity, they can be a real nice dog. They're rough, and enjoy combat and roughhousing. Shepherds guard because they've been bred for generations to do it and have the attitude of 'that's my job,' but a pit bull has a more natural aggressive temperament for it.

"Dobermans: More erratic, and not a dog that should be owned by everyone. Some people who drive a car aren't geared for handling a high-speed sports car. A Doberman isn't necessarily the guard dog for everyone either.

"Labrador retrievers: They're a friendly dog who will be protective of their own property and people. Labradors can be trained for attack work, and still be good pets for children.

"Terriers are good because small dogs with a high activity level who bark a lot have the right characteristics for watchdogs. Terriers'

277 Secrets Your Dog Wants You to Know

Fighting Cats and Dogs

Cat owners have been getting their dander up over who is top dog or top cat for decades. They smugly point out that while there may be fifty-three million dogs in the United States, there are fifty-seven million cats in America.

But according to the American Veterinary Medical Association, Center for Information Management, 36.5 percent of American households own at least one dog and only 30.9 percent own at least one cat.

Furthermore, dog owners spend *twice as much* annually for food, supplies and health care as cat owners, so dog lobbyists have a great deal more clout than the cat people.

Now, what happens with the 14 percent of households in America that have both a cat and a dog?

barks are bigger than their size and they're feisty. That's fine for most; you don't want to rip the mailman to shreds.

"**Poodles** are extremely intelligent, which makes them good as guard dogs, rather than any aggression that's been bred into the dog. The standard poodle works out well when attack-trained. While the smaller ones don't have the weight to mount an effective attack, they're fearless. Even tiny toy poodles will charge a burglar."

The 5 Most Difficult Dogs to Own

The *Chicago Tribune* asked several behaviorists and dog trainers which breeds they believed were the toughest to own.

AKITA: Males can be especially aggressive. One of the trainers told the writer of this story, Steven Dale, that, "Owning an Akita is like dating a psychotic model." (Note: another source on Akitas says they have forty-four documented genetic diseases.)

CHOW CHOW: It's an extremely territorial and aggressive dog, and won't tolerate kids hugging them.

DALMATIAN: People buy one expecting something else because of the adorable picture Disney portrayed. But dalmatians may suffer from many physical ailments, including progressive deafness, according to the story, which appeared on November 29, 1992. Other sources say they're difficult to handle, tempermental, and they shed.

ROTTWEILER: May challenge its owner.

CHINESE SHARPEI: This dog is leery of strangers, moody, with hard-to-read emotions.

Of course, if you have one of these dogs he may be wonderful and never cause you any problems. Alas, others have found that owning one requires extra patience, money, professional trainers, and liability insurance.

How to Diet with Your Dog

Is it difficult to feel ribs when running your hands down the sides? Is getting enough exercise a problem? Is there a lot of eating in between meals or going for foods that one shouldn't? Does the abdomen hang over or is clearly visible? Is there shortness of breath after running a short distance?

If the answers are yes for you *and* your dog, both of you better diet. The figure generally given is that half of all dogs in America are obese. There is also an English study showing that, at least over there, fat people tend to have portly pups.

Both of you may have already tried to go on a diet—and failed. After all, it's a dog-eat-nosh world, and few owners can resist giving their best friends some tasty between-meal treats. Furthermore, some pet foods, like people foods, are often too high in fat. The more fat in the food, the better he likes it. Sound familiar, eh?

Some of the dangers of obesity appear to be the same for people and dogs: heart and respiratory problems; difficulties with blood sugar levels; gastrointestinal disorders; and skeletal stress. Too much weight may also be a contributing factor to a dog's arthritis, diabetes, decreased resistance to infectious diseases, and an increased risk when anesthetized. All of which can lead to a shorter life.

Still, the two of you can try to diet together, using some of the same techniques that work for people.

1. **Fill up on bulk**. There are high-fiber dog and people foods, which provide a feeling of fullness with little fat.

2. **Don't change to a low fat diet all at once.** Gradually convert, so both of you have a chance to get used to it.

3. **Frequent feedings.** Three or four small meals a day may help reduce hunger pangs.

Jogging with Your Dog

Jogging with your dog is a terrific way for you both to exercise, but follow these safety tips offered by Purina Pet Foods:

- Keep your dog on a leash when running so that you are in control.
- Avoid concrete and blacktop in the warmer months, because road surfaces get too hot for the pads on your dog's paws.
- If you are running in the street, face the traffic, with your dog in heel position on your left.
- Give your dog water every twenty minutes on warm days.
- Let him set the pace, and run with a slack leash.

4. **Avoid crash diets**. They're dangerous for both of you.

5. **Keep a written record of weight loss**. Set a goal and note the pattern of eating when it shouldn't occur.

6. **Eliminate unplanned snacks.** Your record should include the time and place for meals, and you should stick to it. Both of you should stay away from the kitchen and dining area when you're not eating a regularly scheduled meal.

7. **Carrots and celery are good for both of you**. They're healthful fillers that don't add calories or cause problems for either of you. Chop them up really fine and mix it in with his food. Or grind it so your dog will easily chew it.

8. **Exercise more**. If you normally walk your dog twice a day, try to make it three times. If you usually go to the end of the block, go to the one beyond that.

9. **Use nonfood treats for rewards**. When you lose weight, let yourself read for an extra hour. Buy your dog a new toy, or spend extra time massaging him.

10. **Avoid diet pills.** They're bad for both of you.

How to Stop Two Dogs from Fighting

If your dog is suddenly attacked by another dog, or vice versa, don't try to stop the fight by pulling their faces apart or grabbing the collar of your dog, or the other dog, or both. Putting your hands anywhere near the front of two fighting dogs' faces makes you likely to be bitten, which could become very dangerous if the other dog is a stray.

If the dog is being walked, however, the best way for you both to stop your dogs is to each grab your dogs' back legs and pull on the legs to separate them, suggests George Whitney, D.V.M. This is easiest to do if you throw your jacket over their heads.

His other tips include:

- Grab the tail of your dog and pull. This is not always possible with many breeds, and may not work for a large dog.

- If the dog isn't too large, or if you're very strong, you can try lifting the dog off the ground and swinging him around. Just throw him away from the other dog and yell at him at the same time.

- If there's a hose anywhere nearby, squirting them will usually stop them.

- If you're near a garbage can, bang the cover with a stick, as near to them as you dare get.

- Throw a blanket over them.

Dr. Whitney mentioned that the above may not work with certain breeds. For example, "Pit bulls and terriers bred for fighting are trained not to stop fighting regardless of what is done to them." So if doing something like banging garbage cans is just music to their ears, there's something else you can do.

Stopping Your Own Dogs from Fighting

When you bring a second dog into your house, the new dog may eventually vie for top-dog status. To find out how to keep your two dogs from fighting, dog trainer Carol Lea Benjamin says: "If no one is going to get hurt, let the dogs work it out themselves. Only interfere if one of them is going to send the other out for stitches," advises this trainer, illustrator, and author of several books, including *Surviving Your Dog's Adolescence*.

To prevent many squabbles in the first place: "I always feed the original dog first. I give him his toy first, and I walk him first if they're walked separately. That's the way not to have jealousy and fights."

She says that you can stop a fight once it's starting if you have taught your dogs that you're boss. For example, when you initiate eye contact, they know that you're in control. "I feel that the most important issue is not who's dominant among the dogs, but that they know *you* are dominant and in charge."

"If they're properly trained," she continues, "they'll stop fighting if you get their attention when you give them the 'eye.' That says, 'No matter who is up or down among you, I'm so far above you that you don't do anything without my approval. And I certainly don't approve of my own dogs fighting with each other.'"

NOTE: To avoid fights in the first place, she says to get opposite sex dogs that tend not to fight with each other.

You surely won't *want* to, however; in fact, you may not even want to *read* this paragraph if you're squeamish. Dr. Whitney says, "Trainers stop these fights by inserting a finger into the dog…and twisting their finger and digging it into the lining of the dog, which causes the dog to release its hold." Don't say we didn't warn you.

Whatever you do, or don't do, the important thing, says Whitney, is to work on the winning dog—the attacker—not the losing one, because you'll have a better chance of putting an end to the fight. "If you take the side of the loser, the winner will come after him. Psychologically with dogs, you take the side of the victor."

Dr. J. Michael Cornwell, the dog bite expert from Glencoe, Ohio,

Simple Trick Stops Dogs from Biting

Biting dogs are sometimes put to sleep, but a simple alternative method for euthanasia in these instances might be considered.

Joseph Stuart, D.V.M., has had success with reducing biting dogs' canine teeth down to—or just below—the level of their incisors. He did this at his Little River Veterinary Clinic in Fairfax, Virginia, and his technique was reported in *Pet Behavior Newsletter*. Stuart claimed positive results in "preventing foxhounds from fighting, and a Saint Bernard and cocker spaniel from biting."

Dr. Stuart asserts that the treatment causes no adverse side effects. Afterwards, dogs eat normally, and there is no increase in dental decay. Of course, the dog's face may look a little funny.

thinks it is a good idea to "throw a jacket between the dogs, or use a tree branch, or grab a broom and either stick it between them or swat one on the fanny." But the important thing to watch out for, he cautioned, was "redirected aggression. In a fighting frenzy, the aggression is so pent up, and the dogs are so wired up that either one of the dogs could turn on you—including your own. If you become involved, be aware that you're always risking either dog turning on you."

Why Christmas May Not Be So Merry for Your Dog

Deck the halls with boughs of holly—but watch out for the berries if you've got a dog. And, 'tis the season to be jolly—but not always for your dog, who risks a number of holiday hazards.

For example, those Yule logs on the fire may look warm, but flying embers could make it dangerous if they singe or burn his coat. Your dog can also burn his paws if he gets too close to the fire.

There may be gifts under the tree for the rest of your family, but for your dog it may be danger that lurks there, especially if you've received edible presents like chocolate. And danger doesn't only hide *under* the tree. What if your dog brushes by it (or God forbid tries to urinate on the trunk!) and knocks it over? Or eats the tinsel, which Dr. John Rush at Tufts University School of Veterinary Medicine warns can saw right through dogs' intestines as they try to pass it. Then there are Christmas plants like poinsettia, not to mention all those tempting foods around—most of which aren't good for him.

Your dog may also find plenty of bad things to eat, and we already discussed the dangers of turkey skin, bones, twine, or thermometers. But even if *you're* careful, your house or dieting dinner guests may slip your dog foods that are too high in fat for them—and for your dog. Like the fat from the ham, or the cookies they're trying not to touch. Or, perhaps they (or their children) think it's cute to give your dog lots of alcohol, like eggnog, and your dog becomes comatose. Dogs can die from alcohol intoxication if they drink enough.

Guests can also upset your dog's normal routine. Richard Molay, a humorist and dog writer described in *Good Dog!* the work a dog has to do when guests arrive. "First they have to be barked at from the moment they approach the driveway. Then, they have to be sniff-inspected for concealed weapons (and cookies). Finally, they have to be licked when they sit down on the sofa. A large dinner party can exhaust a small dog."

Another problem is that not all guests can tolerate dogs. Your pup may have added stresses by being banished someplace, (no) thanks to an allergic mother-in-law or anti-dog college chum.

With all these things transpiring, your dog may need *more* attention than usual—but you probably have less free time during the busy holiday season.

Here are a few ways to prevent Christmas from turning out to be "bark humbug" for your dog and you.

- When you leave a room with a Christmas tree, unplug the lights and be sure your dog is out of there.

- Keep the screen up in front of the fireplace.

- Ask your guests not to feed your dog and watch what goodies *you* give him.

- Be extra watchful of his environment, especially if you have candles and decorations.

Safe Christmases are merry Christmases for your dog.

16 Secrets to Help You Pick Your Next Puppy

You can't pick your relatives but you can choose your dog. And you should pick that puppy very carefully because, hopefully, you'll have him for a long time. Dr. Steven Radbill and others offer some tips to people buying a puppy, as well as to new breeders, who may find some of this helpful in selling their dogs.

- Look above the paw for the bump where the dog's wrist will be. The growth plate of the puppy's leg bones will grow upward from this point. If he or she is going to be very large when fully grown, this plate will be quite prominent.

- Pick up a pinch of skin on his back and release it. The flesh should quickly return to its original shape. If not, the dog may be dehydrated—a symptom of several illnesses.

- Look at his belly. A pot-bellied stomach tells you a dog probably has worms.

- Look at his gums. Pale, cold gums may be a sign of some problem involving blood loss.

- Look at his skin. Dandruff and/or dryness of the coat may indicate a long-standing illness.

- Pick him up. If he cries, he may have trouble bonding with people.

- Avoid a pup that plays too hard or is too aggressive. You may regret it later.

- Try to select a puppy who's neither the dominant nor the submissive one in the litter. He'll be easier to train and discipline with a more pleasing personality.

2 Great Ideas for Training Puppies

Having trouble getting your puppy to urinate directly on the paper? In the video "Good Owners, Great Dogs," trainer Brian Kilcommons suggests that you take a piece of newspaper your pup has already dampened, and place that in the center of the new newspaper, under the top layer. Your dog will be attracted to the scent and urinate right over it, rather than on the sides of the paper, where it may spill over onto your floor.

He also offers a solution to another type of paper problem: dogs unrolling toilet paper. If your puppy likes to do this, balance an empty can with some pennies in it on top of the roll. The next time your pup unravels the paper, the can will fall down and the noise may discourage him from continuing his little game.

We asked Brian how many pennies one should use and he said fifteen were good, but that "one shouldn't be compulsive about it." Then why fifteen? "Otherwise, some use two and some use three hundred," he said.

- Look at the size of his feet. A puppy with really large feet could turn out to be gigantic, although there isn't always a connection.

- Lift his tail. Make sure there's no diarrhea residue. If there is, he could be a sickly dog.

- Get it in writing that you can return the dog within 72 hours if there's a health problem. Then, take the dog to a vet for a health checkup before you make a final decision. Veterinarians can warn people of certain problems with some dogs.

- Ask the breeder for his opinion as to which dog is best for you. He's spent the last few months with the pups and knows them well.

- Ask to see the dam of the litter. This will give you an idea of what the dog will look like when full-grown.

How Much Does That Doggie in Your House Cost?

The following table, put together by the Humane Society of the United States, includes many expenses you may *not* incur, such as boarding, training, and if you're lucky, flea and tick care. Even so, they say the first year's cost of a dog could easily total over $1,000. Here's a simplified breakdown with average prices:

- Adoption from a shelter—$55
- Vaccinations for first year—$200; $65 for each following year
- Toys and grooming supplies—$160
- Grooming—up to $50/visit
- Boarding—$300 for a ten- to fourteen-day stay
- Feeding—varies from $115 to $400 annually
- Training—$50 to $100 annually
- Other vet care—$135 annually
- Flea and tick care—$80 annually

- If you're in a private breeding establishment, don't take him—or any of their dogs—if the dog is coughing. The pup could have a highly contagious kennel cough.

Famous dog trainer and author of three books and one video-tape, Brian Kilcommons, who appears regularly on Lifetime Television's *Our Home* show, and is a consultant for the Tufts University School of Veterinary Medicine, said you should also:

- Turn the puppy over as if you're cradling a baby. If he screams and tries to right himself, he may be unstable.
- If you have children at home, gently squeeze the skin between the dog's toes. Your kids will probably do a lot worse, so you should determine your puppy's pain tolerance now.

Dogs Need Sunscreen, Too!

Dogs, like humans, can suffer from sunstroke, sun poisoning, sunburns and skin cancer—four good reasons not to leave them to swelter without shelter for any period of time. Veterinarians are also reporting an increase in skin cancers these days, partially as a result of the depletion of the ozone layer.

These dangerous and disfiguring skin cancers most often appear on the ears, nose, around the eyes, or on a sun-bathed stomach. "Your dog is at special risk if he has a large pink area around his nose, is hairless, or has a long nose, like a beagle or a collie," says Richard W. Greene, D.V.M., of the Manhattan Veterinary Group.

Other sun-related problems can also lead to cancer. Dogs can get something similar to sun poisoning in human beings, whereby unpigmented noses may become red, puffy, and sore. This condition, called "collie nose," can also lead to skin cancer, says Dr. Greene, who some consider to be the best animal surgeon in America. He states that sunburns are another danger for dogs—especially for white ones like dalmatians and white bull terriers—and repeated sunburns can again lead to cancer.

Here are some ideas he suggested for protecting your dog in the sun:

1. Use waterproof SPF 15 sunblock on the exposed areas of his skin when he's outside in the sun. Don't bother putting it on his fur; it won't add any protection and he'll probably just lick it off. Ask your vet what brand of sunscreen is best, because some dogs are allergic to certain ingredients.

2. Don't walk your dog in the hot sun for long. Early in the morning and in the cool part of the evening is best.

3. Keep your dog under an umbrella at the beach.

Bow-Focals for Your Dog

Like people, dogs can wear "glasses," and get cataracts, which can lead to blindness, if untreated. IOL International, Inc. of Largo, Florida, manufactures machines that make these "intraocular canine lenses," which have to be surgically implanted. The lenses cost about $80, and the surgery, done by one's own veterinarian or a specialist, costs between $1,500 and $2,000.

Surprisingly, according to the owner of the company, Gary Goins, only a small percentage of dog owners choose to save their dog's sight with surgery. "For the kind of money an operation costs, most of the owners let their dogs go blind," he says.

4. Make sure he has plenty of fresh water available whenever he's in the sun for more than a few minutes.

5. If your dog stays outside, make sure he has some kind of enclosure with a roof over it. The best color for a doghouse is white.

6. Never keep a dog inside a car when it's hot outside. The sun may not be on the car when you leave, but it can shift quickly. Furthermore, you may think you're only going to spend a few minutes away, but you may bump into a friend, get delayed in a line, or forget about your dog and wander off.

7. If you leave your dog indoors when you go out to work, leave the air-conditioning on for him.

8. As for sunglasses, they *are* good for dogs. But anyone unconventional enough to buy a pair, and actually put them on his or her dog, soon learns the dog will probably only keep them on for a few minutes. (Long enough, we hope, to take a cute photograph.)

9. Watch out for jogging on a hot day. Dogs can't sweat out body heat like humans, and can collapse from a long-distance run.

10. Finally, take your dog to the vet immediately if you notice any skin problems.

Vacationing with Your Dog:
10 Places That Really Want Him

Here are a few ideas for your next vacation, where your dog will be treated the way he should be treated—not like a dog.

Best Hotels

The **Four Seasons** hotels throughout the country give you nothing to growl about. For example:

Ritz-Carlton in Chicago. Actually a Four Seasons hotel, they have an on-premise kennel with grooming, dog walking, "gourmet" room service, etc. (312) 266-1000.

Four Seasons Clift House in San Francisco. Spuds McKenzie's favorite hotel, where, among other canine amenities, they send your dog a personalized welcoming note. (415) 775-4700.

The Pierre in Manhattan gives dogs a wicker bed basket with Italian linen mattress covers and bone-shaped biscuits with their name spelled out in edible icing. (212) 838-8000.

Four Seasons Hotel in Washington, D.C. Go on your dog's birthday and they'll give him a beef-patty birthday cake. (202) 342-0444.

Loews L'Enfant Plaza Hotel in Washington, D.C., is not a Four Seasons hotel, but they'll pamper your pet anyway with dog bones on a silver tray and more. Laudably, their VIP (Very Important Pet) Program donates 5 percent of its earnings to the Washington Humane Society. (202) 484-1000.

River Run Bed and Breakfast. A bed-and-breakfast that likes dogs is located in River Run in Fleischmann's, NY, in the Catskill Mountains. Forty percent of the guests come with their own dog, and those who don't can borrow Ruffian, the cocker spaniel "house dog." (914) 254-4884.

Lorelei Resort in Treasure Island, FL, has a groom-mobile, photographers, pet sitters and a veterinarian on call 24 hours. (800) 35-GO DOG.

Rent-a-Dog!

Renting a best friend by the hour may be the perfect solution to a small apartment, restrictive lease, or not having the time or inclination to walk a dog.

This leash-leasing is going on in Japan, where, according to the *Wall Street Journal*, a Japanese pet shop provides canine company for $10 to $20 an hour, depending on the size of the dog. The shop has a Maltese, a Shih Tzu, a golden retriever and a dozen other breeds available for the dog deprived. In addition to profiting from the rental money, the shop owners benefit by not having to walk their own dogs!

Cypress Inn in Carmel, CA, is co-owned by dog lover/activist Doris Day and permits dogs in guest rooms as well as the public areas and court yards. (800) 443-7443.

Best Ship

Total deck-adence! On the *QE2*, during transatlantic crossings, your dog can stay in a temperature-controlled kennel, run on the Pooches' Promenade, and be cared for by kennel mates. Best of all, he can see you during kennel hours. They also have a dog walking service if you become too involved with everything else that's happening on board. Cunard Line (800) 528-6273.

Best Airline Gimmick

Carnival Airlines, out of Miami, has a frequent pet program: fly ten times with your dog (in or out of the cabin) and they'll give him a free flight. (800) 437-2110.

Best Travel Publication

DogGone: A newsletter so good it will leave you drooling. Bimonthly, with up-to-date information on traveling with your dog and travel-related products for him. Subscription is $24 annually. DogGone, P.O. Box 651155, Vero Beach, FL 32965.

Bone Voyage!

Which States Have the Most Dogs?

According to the AVMA Center for Information Management, people in the Southwest have the most dogs in America per capita. Individual states with the largest percentage of dog-owning households (44 percent or more) are:

- Arkansas
- Nevada
- New Mexico
- Oklahoma
- Texas
- West Virginia
- Wyoming

The largest dog populations are in the following states:

- California (more than 5.7 million)
- Texas (more than 4.5 million)
- New York (more than 2.7 million)
- Florida (2.4 million)
- Ohio (2.2 million)
- Pennsylvania (2.2 million)
- Illinois (2.2 million)

Plants That Can Poison Your Dog

Your dog can be in danger from common household or garden plants—even though they may seem perfectly safe. For example, "nontoxic" plants may be sprayed with insecticides and fetilizers, or a dog left alone in a yard may chew poisonous vegetation or dig up flower bulbs that can harm him.

The first step toward protecting your dog is to be careful about what you buy. There are enough nontoxic plants and flowers to choose from if you place the life of your dog over the beauty of your home or garden.

Even if you make the right choice, though, and you think there can't possibly be any risk, safe unsprayed plants can still cause occasional problems. Like irritation to the dog's mouth from sap. Or situations similar to what happened in Louisiana where a woman lost her dog after he chewed on banana tree stalks in her yard and suffered a major internal blockage.

Another danger outside may come from something as seemingly innocuous as placing a dog's bowl under a tree for shade. One has to consider the potential danger of acorns falling from the trees, according to Gus Thornton, D.V.M., writing in the Massachusetts SPCA's *Animals* magazine.

Even though acorns aren't poisonous, they could cause an obstruction that might have to be removed surgically. Of course putting your dog under something like a *coconut* tree could present an altogether different type of hazard!

To tell you some of the plants you should avoid if you have dogs, and their effects, Joel Rapp, "Mr. Mother Earth," has put together the list below. Mr. Rapp, who lives in Los Angeles, is a world-renowned gardening expert, columnist, and an author (*Mr. Mother Earth's Hassle-Free Indoor Plant Book*) who is familiar to viewers of the television programs *Live with Regis and Kathie Lee* and *Mike and Maty*.

Food Odors Dogs Like Best

Dogs decide what foods they like by the odor, so the smells of twenty-six foods were tested by the College of Veterinary Medicine at Texas A&M University. Dr. Bonnie Beaver found that liver and chicken ranked highest over everything else, such as fresh fruit, fish, hamburgers, and vegetables.

In other food tests, summarized in *Applied Animal Behaviour Science* (volume 34, 1992), dogs preferred canned and cooked meat over raw, and warm and moist food to cold and dry.

ALOE VERA: diarrhea, change of urine color to red

AMARYLLIS: vomiting

ASPARAGUS FERN: might cause allergic dermatitis

AUTUMN CROCUS: the leaves cause vomiting and nervous stimulation

AVOCADO: vomiting, diarrhea, and possible death

AZALEA: depression of the central nervous system and cardiovascular collapse

BIRD OF PARADISE: gastrointestinal disorders, vertigo

CYCLAMEN: vomiting, gastrointestinal problems, death

DAFFODIL: convulsions, vomiting, arrhythmia

DUMB CANE: the various dieffenbachia plants can cause oral irritation, leading to suffocation

EASTER LILY: kidney failure

FRUIT AND NUT TREES: like apple, peach, almond, cherry, and apricot, which have stems and leaves with traces of cyanide

HIBISCUS: gastrointestinal reactions

HOLLY: vomiting, diarrhea, and central nervous system depression

HYDRANGEA: similar to fruit trees

LILY OF THE VALLEY: cardiac failure

MISTLETOE: cardiac problems

MORNING GLORY: depression or hyperactivity

NIGHTSHADE: solanine in plant causes salivation, anorexia, gastrointestinal disturbance, depression

PHILODENDRON: calcium oxalate crystals lead to oral and gastrointestinal irritation

POINSETTIA: irritating to mouth, stomach, and possibly the heart

RHODODENDRON: same as azalea

RHUBARB: leave can kill dogs

SCHEFFLERA: see philodendron

TOBACCO: leaves cause nervous stimulation

TOMATO: leaves and stems contain solanine; same as nightshade

VEGETABLES: such as eggplant, mushrooms, toadstools, and potatoes, may cause vomiting and diarrhea

The 50 Words Your Dog May Know—and How to Increase His Intelligence

One day, when we were going over the spices that would be in a dinner dish, we mentioned cumin. Immediately our two teacup Shih Tzus leaped to the door and started barking. We were mystified until we realized that they thought we had said "come in," and were trying to welcome our "visitors."

Experts believe that some dogs, particularly poodles and dogs bred for sheep herding, can understand hundreds of words. But the vocabulary of most dogs is far smaller than that. To find out which words dogs were most likely to know, we interviewed fifty Long Island dog owners. Alas, we found that—based on reports by their owners—few untrained non-guard pet dogs were able to understand even twenty words.

Had we included the sounds they understood, however, like keys jingling, or our body language they responded to, such as picking up a leash, or odors they recognized, including those of different family members, it would have been different. English dog behaviorists like Barbara Woodhouse believe that a smart dog may respond to as many as four hundred words or stimuli.

Additionally, dogs have their own "vocabularies" that enable them to communicate with each other, with us, and with other animals. This includes numerous body language signals, and many kinds of barks, pants, and howls.

Here are the words we found to be most often recognized by dogs. Stars indicate that most dogs knew these words, according to their proud owners.

1. Baby
2. Bad★
3. Ball
4. Bark
5. Bath
6. Beach

7. Bed

8. Bone

9. Can (food)

10. Car*

11. Cat

12. Chair

13. Come*

14. Couch

15. Daddy

16. Dinner

17. Dog

18. Door

19. Drop

20. Eat*

21. Fetch

22. Food* (type they like, e.g., biscuit, chicken)

23. Get

24. Go

25. Good*

26. House (or home)

27. Hurry

28. I (me, owner's name)

29. Kiss

30. Leash

31. Let's go _____ (eat, whatever)

32. Lie (down)

33. Mommy

34. Name* (his, family members, and/or other pets in house)

35. No*

36. Off

37. Out*

38. Paw

39. Quiet

40. Run

41. Sit*

42. Sleep

43. Stay*

44. Stick

45. Toy (including name and/or type)

46. Treat

47. Up

48. Walk*

49. Water

50. Yes

The 10 Smartest Dog Breeds

Dr. Stanley Coren named the Border collie, poodle, German shepherd, golden retriever, Doberman pinscher, Shetland sheep dog, Labrador retriever, papillon, rottweiler and Australian cattle dog as the top ten breeds in obedience and working intelligence.

This caused a great howl to go up from those whose dogs landed at the tail of the list. Owners of borzois, chow chows, bulldogs, basenjis and Afghan hounds insisted that their dogs weren't dumb at all; they were just too smart to do Coren's stupid tests.

On Charlie Rose's television show, Dr. Coren told how he handled offended dog owners, recalling what he told an Afghan owner: "You have beautiful dogs.... They are quite spectacular...." He found this mollified people because, "We prize beauty and aesthetics in our culture as much as we do intelligence."

As for increasing your dog's intelligence, British Columbia psychology professor Stanley Coren, author of *The Intelligence of Dogs*, speaking on the *Charlie Rose* show on April 13, 1994 said: "One of the simple things to do is to talk to the dog...using consistent language, and I don't mean...love talk.... If you say to the dog each time you're going to go out of the house 'Let's go out...' or 'Do you want a cookie?'...whenever you're going to be giving them [one] treat...after a while the dog is going to learn that those sounds...and those wavings of the hand mean something. And that's the first step...because a lot of...dogs [don't] know that you're trying to communicate."

How to Get Your Dog to Do What You Want

We asked Warren Eckstein, well-known animal behaviorist, television- and radio personality, and author of five books, exactly what he meant by the title of his current book: *How to Get Your Dog to Do What You Want*.

"You can't take an animal into a human environment, treat it like an animal, and expect it to respond like part of the family," he said. "You've got to treat it like part of the family to get that response."

The problem is: what member of the family will decide the dog's role or place. "The husband says to the dog 'Jump up' on the bed, and the wife says 'Sleep in the other room,' and the dog is going to be confused.

"Decide in advance with other family members what your expectations are for your pet," he advises. "Can he sleep in bed with you? Is he allowed on the furniture? Then, everyone in the family can establish a consistent approach with the dog, he won't get mixed messages, and he will do what you want—all the time, not sporadically."

How to Have Your Dog Cared for After You Die

More than one million pets in America have supposedly been named as beneficiaries in their owners' wills. Some people have even named *other* people's dogs in their wills. A woman in England has left $30,000 to Queen Elizabeth's corgis, but not any money to her only child, because the woman believes she's a poor relative of the royal family.

Here are ten sensible things you should know about preparing now for what can happen to your dog after you die:

1. If you have to leave your dog to a shelter, you might want to consider a no-kill shelter, which doesn't euthanize their dogs. For a directory of these places, send $15 to Lynda J. Foro, c/o No-Kill Directory, P.O. Box 10905, Glendale, AZ 85318.

Before you assume that this is the best place for your dog, consider that while no-kill shelters are a wonderful *idea*, unfortunately not enough people in this world have the wonderful notion of adopting second-hand dogs, especially older ones. Sally Fekety at the Humane Society says: "It may take a long time to place your dog in a home from these shelters, if at all. It might languish in a crate the rest of its life because no one takes him in. Would you really want that for your dog?"

2. We're sure no one reading a book like this would ever consider having their dog put to sleep when they die, but we just wanted to tell you that such requests have not been carried out by the courts anyway.

3. Another solution that may not work is advertising to give your dog away after you die. Ms. Fekety warns: "Some people who answer these classified advertisements pose as buyers, sometimes even coming along with a child, and they promise to give the dog a loving home. Then they sell it for research or worse. It's

We Kill 7 Dogs Per Minute

"About seven dogs are killed in animal shelters every minute," says Rachel Lamb, director of Companion Animal Care for the Humane Society of the United States in Washington, D.C. "Some are lost pets whose owners can't be found. Others are pets whose owners can no longer keep them. Not enough people choose to adopt them," she adds sadly.

Here are some more upsetting statistics about this situation:

- At least one-fourth of all animals in shelters are purebreds.
- Half the animals brought to most shelters are euthanized.
- It costs an average of $100 for them to handle an animal.
- Fifty-five hundred pets are born every hour in the United States.
- One female dog and her offspring can produce 67,000 dogs in six years. So if you won't spay or neuter your nonbreeding dog for *his* or *her* sake, consider the *world's*.

easier for thieves to get dogs this way than to run the risk of stealing an animal and being seen."

4. The best solution is to find a friend or relative *now* who will agree to take your dog after you die. Discuss it with him or her *now* rather than surprising them in your will, because they may not want or be able to take him. They may be more sanguine about the whole situation if you leave them some money for food, squeaky toys, and veterinary expenses for the rest of your dog's probable life.

5. You can also leave money to your veterinarian and have him arrange for your dog to be cared for after you die. But again, no surprises. Discuss this all with him in advance. You may wish to leave him any remaining money when your dog dies, or arrange to have it go to somebody else or some organization. Have your lawyer draw up the contract. A sample veterinary contract can be found in *Dog Law* by Mary Randolph.

6. Never leave money directly to your dog. He won't get it, and you can bet that some relative, no matter how remote, is going to sue. Then the money could end up with an alternate beneficiary or that dog-hating cousin you always despised. You can have your lawyer draw up your will.

7. Most states don't allow trusts for animals. But would you want one? Attorney Mary Randolph writes: "Dogs can't go to court to snitch on a dishonest or inept trustee who spends the dog chow money on lottery tickets."

8. There are a few places that will take care of your dog if you leave them a large sum of money, say $25,000 or so, such as the Companion Animal Geriatric Center at Texas A&M. Ask your veterinarian or local Humane Society to help you find one of these places.

9. There are also a number of shelters and rescue groups that help save specific types of dogs, such as a pedigree or a therapy dog. For a list of breed and rescue groups, consult *The Canine Sourcebook*, by Susan Bulanda.

There are also many organizations (PAWS, POWARS, Pet Pals, Pet Support Network, etc.) that specifically help pets of people with AIDS. There is no central registry for these groups, so call your local AIDS organization for more information.

10. Instead of leaving your money to a dog, if you decide to leave it to an organization that helps other dogs, or animals, the organization may help you find your dog a happy home after you die.

How to Give Your Dog
a Nose-to-Toes Examination

Yes, you can and should give your dog regular at-home check-ups, but they should *not* be a substitute for a thorough examination at least once a year by your veterinarian. Still, a monthly five-minute exam could enable you to catch something you'd have missed waiting a year between visits.

The following suggestions for how to do this were given by Amy Marder, V.M.D., author of a regular pet column in *Prevention*, and a book called *Your Healthy Pet*.

First, look at your dog generally for any obvious swellings or discharges. Is his hair coming out? Does his coat have a nice sheen to it?

Then, feel his entire body, including the abdomen, for lumps, bumps, or areas that seem painful to your dog, such as his joints.

Feel his ribs and see if he seems to have lost or gained weight since the last time you did this.

Lift up the side of his mouth. Are his teeth clean? Is his breath bad? If so, he could have dental problems (or, less likely, kidney or digestive problems). Also see if he has healthy-looking pink gums. Pale gums can mean anemia; bluish gums, respiratory or heart ailments; yellowish gums, possible liver trouble; and red irritated gums, dental disease. Also, check his tongue for lumps.

Look at his eyes and see if there are any discharges. Are they red? If you have a small flashlight, you can shine it into each eye to see if the pupil constricts (becomes smaller). Note also if he turns away or starts blinking or tearing when you shine the light in his eye. If he does, he may have a problem. Look at his nose. Is it nice and wet? Is there any discharge coming from it?

Lift up his ear flaps. Are they pinkish as they should be, or are they red? Are there any bites or swellings inside or outside of his ears? Do you see any debris that needs to be cleaned out?

Reasons People Take Their Pets to the Vet

According to the American Animal Hospital Association, the following were the reasons fourteen hundred people took their pets to the vet:

1. Vaccinations and exams (87 percent)

2. Care for sick pet (58 percent)

3. Surgery (38 percent)

4. To buy food and vitamins (32 percent)

5. Dentistry (29 percent)

6. Flea treatments (21 percent)

7. Care for injured pet (18 percent)

8. Boarding (18 percent)

9. Grooming (10 percent)

10. Euthanasia (9 percent)

Look at his toes. Do his nails need clipping? Is there any rash in between his toes? Make sure to also check his back paws between the pads to see if there are any foreign bodies stuck in there.

Lift up his tail and look at his rear end to see if there's any pasted stool, which is an indication of diarrhea.

Look to see if there is a discharge from the vulva or penis. If he has testicles, note any lumps or note any changes in size.

Finally, remember to praise him for being so good while you did all this to him. And if you did encounter any problems, do not attempt to treat them yourself but seek professional help.

Could Your Dog Pass a
Good Citizen Test?

For a dog to be a good citizen doesn't mean that he knows how to vote, or that he knows the names of the presidents and their dogs (and cats!). "It means that the dog has passed the Canine Good Citizen Test, a series of simple behavior tests that are mostly a matter of manners," says Pennsylvania writer Sherry Carpenter, who is the best-known advocate of this American Kennel Club program, and regularly writes columns on it for *Dog World*.

"Life is full of surprises and your dog should respond calmly to most of them," says Ms. Carpenter, who stresses that being a good citizen could one day save a dog's life. For example, "A landlord may insist that a badly behaved dog leave the building, and the owner may have to send him to a shelter. Or a dog who responds badly to sudden stimuli may run away and be hit by a car."

Here is a reduced version of the AKC-approved Canine Good Citizen Test. How many of these can your dog pass?

- Is your dog clean, groomed, healthy, and up to date on his license and rabies vaccination?

- Would he act courteously in the presence of a stranger who talks to you and ignores him?

- Can he walk on a loose lead (staying on your left side)?

- Can he walk through a crowd without straining at the leash or showing resentment or shyness?

- Will he sit and allow a stranger to pet him?

- Can he sit and get down on command?

- Will he then stay or sit in position?

- If two other people and their dogs came nearby and chatted, would he stay with you, or go to—or bark at—the other dog?

The Real Reason People Have Dogs

According to a study done in England, many with companion dogs preferred them to people because dogs were more loyal and faithful; didn't answer back; were more affectionate, reliable, honest, and trustworthy; were better companions; and less selfish and demanding.

In America, Dr. William Kay, chief of staff of the Animal Medical Center in Manhattan, explained why people have dogs in his book, *The Complete Book of Animal Health*:

"The single most fundamental reason for dog ownership is love.... Dogs are true, loyal friends who give their owners and others nonjudgmental persistent affection and love throughout their lives. They are very easy to be with. They never grow up and never grow out of their complete affection, loyalty and love."

- If he saw someone on crutches or in a wheelchair, would he remain confident or start barking?

- Will he stay poised during distractions like the sudden opening or closing of a door? Or the dropping of a large book behind him? Or a jogger, bicyclist, or skater in front of him on the path? Or someone pushing a shopping cart in front of him?

- Can he be left alone for fifteen minutes or so without barking, whining, howling, pacing or getting too upset?

Ms. Carpenter points out, "Training your dog to pass the evaluation gives him an AKC certification that's a lot better than just saying 'My dog is a good dog.' It proves that you're a responsible dog owner."

Furthermore, having a well-behaved dog not only makes him look good, and you look good, "but can help counter the growing anti-animal sentiment," she says.

The 11 Worst Things We Do
to Dogs in This World

It really is a dog-eat-dog world—and in some places, a people-eat-dog world as well. That's just one of the heinous things we do to our best friends. John C. Walsh, international projects director of the World Society for the Protection of Animals, whose headquarters are in Boston, tells some of the ways people are hurting dogs throughout the world.

Eating dogs takes place in Cambodia, Laos, Vietnam, Korea, parts of China, and elsewhere. Sometimes the dogs are put out in open cages at restaurants or markets and killed on the spot. Foreigners don't always know what they're really eating, because dogs may be served in dishes with names like All Season Soup.

Killing of stray dogs with strychnine: The poison, hidden inside a piece of liver, induces agonizing seizures. It causes some dogs to chew their tongues off—and it can take them up to two hours to die.

Electrocution of dogs: For example, in Delhi, India, one thousand dogs are killed each week, slaughtered in primitive electrocution chambers. Most of them are healthy pets, because sick and rabid dogs hide and are rarely caught. Electrocution doesn't kill them immediately. They undergo fifteen to twenty seconds of excruciating pain first.

Dog fights: This is now a worldwide problem. In Russia, two dogs recently fought for more than an hour and had to be regularly doused with water to prevent them from passing out. Even though dog fighting is illegal in America, the promoters don't mind paying fines of $200 to $500 since they may bet something like $2,000, and have a good chance of winning.

To get an aggressive disposition, promoters inbreed the animals to bring out their worst qualities. This can make dogs like pit bulls and Staffordshire terriers ferocious as well as unpredictable in behavior. They may then attack their owners and others, which gives all

Cleveland Amory on How to Help the Homeless (Dog)

We asked Cleveland Amory, the great humorist and humanitarian, what people could do to help dogs without homes.

1. Acquaint yourself with your veterinarian's or animal hospital's policy concerning stray dogs. Some won't look at a homeless or injured animal picked up by a person unless the person has cash. Ask your vet what his office's policy is. Most doctors and lawyers do charity work, but not all vets will. Do you want to continue to go to a vet who doesn't?

2. There are too many animals out there and too few homes. When you want a dog, choose one from a shelter over a breeder. Buying a breeder's or pet store's dog does not help reduce the number who have to be put down. A shelter will not only give you what you want, but also the wonderful feeling that you've saved a dog.

3. When you see a homeless dog, try to save it. If you call an animal control place they may put him down. Call people and try to find that dog a home if you can't take him in yourself.

4. Support your local shelter and a national organization of your choice, both with money and volunteer time.

breeds a bad image, especially those. Then no one wants them and they have to be destroyed.

Puppy mills: Dogs are often badly mistreated, kept in outdoor cages in subzero weather, and piled on each other like cordwood.

Breeding genetically unsound animals: For example, dachshunds with bad backs and German shepherds with hip dysplasia are still bred. Then, after living a short painful life, their owners may abandon them, or they may have to be destroyed, breaking the hearts of the families who have grown to love them.

Breeding animals in one country for misuse elsewhere: In America, pit bull terriers are exported for dog fights in Russia. In Britain (mostly Wales), dogs are being bred to be eaten in countries where that's accepted.

So-called scientific research: Some is done without concern for the animal's suffering, or for alternative research methods. Often the research isn't needed, has been done before, and doesn't prove anything.

Killing war dogs in conflicts: Dogs are used and abused by the military in many ways, such as putting explosives on them and then detonating them.

Extinction of wild dogs all over the world: As one illustration, no ones cares about the African wild dog, and it's now an endangered species.

Greyhound racing: The promoters of this "sport" claim the dogs are sent out to be adopted afterwards. But they often aren't, because the promoters don't want them to be raised to compete with their own dogs. The greyhound rescue groups try to help, but the supply of greyhounds appears to exceed the demand for them.

What can you do to stop these horrors? Walsh says there are seven thousand animal protection groups in this world and most have their own newsletters. Reading these keeps you informed as to what's going on—and how to protest it. Most important, the money from these newsletter subscriptions helps the group fund their programs.

★   ★   ★   ★   ★

We (the authors) have chosen the following worthwhile animal ethics, rights and welfare organizations, all of whom have interesting publications distributed free to members or supporters.

Animal Rights Network, P.O. Box 25881, Baltimore, MD   21224, (410) 675-4566. *The Animals' Agenda*

American Humane Association, 63 Inverness Dr. East, Englewood, CO 80112, (303) 792-9900. *The Advocate*

American Society for the Prevention of Cruelty to Animals, 424 East 92nd St., New York, NY   10128, (212) 876-7711. *Animal Watch*

Delta Society, P.O. Box 1080, Renton, WA   98057, (206) 226-7357. *Interactions* and *Anthrozoos*

Fund for Animals Inc., 200 West 57th St., New York, NY   10019, (212) 246-2096. *Bulletin*

$9,500 in Rewards

The Humane Society of the United States, diligent in its efforts to stop the abuse of animals, has posted the following rewards:

- Up to $2,500 for information leading to the arrest and conviction of any person who organizes, promotes or officiates at dogfights.

- Up to $2,500 for information leading to the arrest and conviction of any person who uses any live animal as a "lure" in the training and racing of greyhounds.

- Up to $2,000 for information leading to the arrest and conviction of any person who willfully poisons, mutilates, or tortures, or attempts to poison, mutilate, or torture, any dog or cat.

- Up to $2,500 for information leading to the arrest and conviction of any wholesale dealer in dogs and cats who knowingly buys or otherwise procures any stolen animal.

Humane Society of the United States, 2100 L St. NW, Washington, DC 20037, (202) 452-1100. *HSUS News* and *Animal Activist Alert!*

Massachusetts Society for the Prevention of Cruelty to Animals, 350 South Huntington Ave., Boston, MA 02130, (617) 522-7400. *Animals*

Morris Animal Foundation, 45 Inverness Dr. East, Englewood, CO 80112, (800) 243-2345. *Companion Animal News*

National Anti-Vivisection Society, 180 North Executive Dr., Brookfield, WI 53005, (800) 888-NAVS. *NAVS Bulletin*

New England Anti-Vivisection Society, 333 Washington St., Ste. 850, Boston, MA 02108, (617) 589-0522. *NEAVES*

People for the Ethical Treatment of Animals (PETA), P.O. Box 42516, Washington, DC 20015, (301) 770-7444. *Animal Times*

World Society for the Protection of Animals, 29 Perkins St., P.O. Box 190, Boston, MA 02130, (617) 522-7000. *Animals International*

18 (Mostly Free) Hotlines
You Can Call for Free Information

Here are some numbers you can call for support and information, including nutritional, behavioral, and emotional advice. In many cases, if you leave a message, they call you back collect.

Behavioral and Health Questions

1. National Animal Poison Control Centers: (800) 548-2423. Located at the College of Veterinary Medicine at the University of Illinois in Urbana. It costs $30 per case and they will help you if your dog is poisoned. Have the following information ready when you call: your name, address, phone; the species, breed, age, sex, and weight of your dog; the poison you believe he has ingested; the problems he is experiencing; and your credit card number. Or call (900) 680-0000. $20 for the first five minutes; $2.95 for each additional minute.

2. San Francisco Behavior Help Line: (415) 554-3075. They may take two days to return your call, which will be collect.

3. Dial-Pet: (312) 342-5738. Tape-recorded messages about pet health, sponsored by the Chicago Public Library. Tapes are approximately five minutes and are on many subjects.

4. Tree House Animal Foundation Pet Care Hotline: (312) 784-5488. Based in Chicago. Call Monday through Saturday, 9 A.M. to 5 P.M. (CT).

5. Behavioral and Training Problem Hotline: (212) 727-7257. Free advice on behavioral and training problems. The best time to call is between 12 P.M. and 2 P.M. Sponsored by the American Dog Trainers Network.

6. Rabies & Rickettsial Disease Hotline: (404) 332-4555. A twenty-four-hour line from the Centers for Disease Control.

277 Secrets Your Dog Wants You to Know

7. Dr. Jim's Pet Lover Helpline: (900) 776-0007. This line costs 97 cents a minute and is included here even though it's a 900 number because his following is large, his advice is excellent, and the list of available topics is extensive. Most recorded announcements are three to five minutes long.

Nutritional Information

8. IAMS Customer Service: (800) 525-IAMS. Based in Ohio. Call Monday through Saturday, 8 A.M. to 8 P.M. (EST).

9. Hills Customers Affairs Department: (800) 445-5777. Based in Kansas. Call Monday through Friday, 7 A.M. to 6 P.M. (CT).

10. Alpo: (800) 366-6033. Based in Minnesota. Call Monday through Friday, 8 A.M. to 5 P.M. (CT).

11. Proplan (Ralston Purina): (800) PRO-PLAN. Based in St. Louis. Call Monday through Friday, 7 A.M. to 7 P.M. (CT).

Other

12. Low-cost spaying and neutering referral service: (800) 248-SPAY. Call Monday through Friday, 9 A.M. to 5 P.M. (EST).

13. Lost & Found Animal Line: (800) 755-8111. Call to report a found dog. They will keep the listing for two weeks. If you've lost a dog, you can call (900) 535-1515, which costs $1.95 per minute. This twenty-four-hour national hotline tracking system is sponsored by Sprint and the American Humane Association.

14. AKC Information Line: (919) 233-9767. Available twenty-four hours a day for questions about dog and litter registration; to place orders for registration materials, books, etc.; to receive breeder referral contact information; and to inquire about general registration, information, and instructions.

Free Phone Counseling Service for People Whose Dogs Have Died

15. Chicago Veterinary Medical Association: (708) 603-3994.

16. University of California at Davis: (916) 752-4200.

17. University of Florida at Gainesville, College of Veterinary Medicine: (904) 392-4700 x4080.

18. Michigan State College of Veterinary Medicine: (517) 432-2696.

Freebies for and about
Your Dog

Two paws up for places that provide free informational brochures about your dog—and one down for those who offer booklets that are just advertising for the product. We went through all the brochures listed below, and these are the ones we think contain enough valuable information to make your item worth sending for.

When writing a company, always state which brochures you want, since some places offer several of them. Enclose a stamped, self-addressed envelope (#10 business size), and allow up to two months to receive them. Promotions change, and while the following were being offered at the end of 1994, they may no longer be available. Finally, if you want more free things for your dog, buy *Free Stuff for Your Pet* by Linda Bowman. Although some of the material in there is now dated, many of the offers and ideas are still good.

Free Food Samples and Coupons

Purina: Call (800) 699-1380 and they'll send you one of four different types of food. (If you think you can call them back three more times and get the other samples, forget it. Their computer knows if you've already called.)

Nature's Recipe: (800) 843-4008. Free sample.

Iams & Eukanuba: (800) 525-4267 No free sample but if you call them they'll send you a $1.00 discount coupon for food along with various booklets.

Hills: (800) 445-5777. $2 food coupons.

Free Dog Newsletter

Pet Pause is a free newsletter appearing inside Doctors Foster and Smith's catalogue, which comes out four times a year. To receive a copy of the catalogue (and *Pet Pause*), call (800) 562-7169.

Free Veterinarian Consultation

You can get your dog questions answered by Doctors Foster or Smith on Tuesday and Thursday 9 a.m. to 12 p.m. CST by calling (715) 369-2022. (Online, the caring and intelligent vets on AOL's Pet Care Forum will answer your pet medical questions free. AOL: (800) 827-6364)

Free Brochures and Booklets

Caring for Your Puppy; The Fat Dog Problem: How to Solve It; and *Switching Pet Foods*. If you request them, they will also send you a few interesting reprints of independent food studies, including *Feeding Puppies: Common Errors, Their Effects, and Prevention; Harmful Effects of Common Dog Feeding Practices*; and *Avoid Problems with Proper Diet*. Hills Pet Nutrition, P.O. Box 148, Topeka, KS 66601.

Enjoy Your Four-Footed Friends; Housing Happy Pets & Happy People: Tenant Guidelines; Housing Happy Pets & Happy People: Management Guidelines. Pet Food Institute, 1200 19th St. NW, Washington, DC 20036.

You and Your New Puppy: A Guide to Proper Care and Training. The Iams Company, 7250 Poe Ave., P.O. Box 14597, Dayton, OH 45413.

Controlling External Parasites, Cold Weather Care of Dogs, Warm Weather Care of Dogs, Building a Doghouse, Building a Whelping Box, Controlling Internal Parasites, A Healthy Start for Your Puppy and *Permanent Identification for Your Dog*. *All About Your Dog*, contains $3.00 in discount coupons for food products. Their *Pet Care Reports*, include *Your Aging Dog*, and *Breaking Dogs' Bad Habits*. Ralston Purina Company, Checkerboard Square, St. Louis, MO 63164.

How to Fly with Your Pet. Humane Society of the United States, 2100 L Street NW, Washington, DC 20037.

My First Puppy; Strangers and the Family Dog; Introducing Your Dog to Your New Baby; Housetraining Puppies and Dogs; Guide to Grooming; How to Control Worms in Dogs; Dealing with Your Overactive Dog; Feeding Your Dog Right; First Aid for Dogs; What Every Good Dog Should Know; The Vaccination Story; Welcoming Your New Puppy; The Brood Bitch and Puppies; The Dog That Cannot Be Left Alone; The Fearful Dog; Easing Its Fright; Caring for the Older Dog, Dealing with Your Overactive Dog; Elimination Problems in Dogs; Fear of Thunder and Other Loud Noises; and Is Your Dog Overweight? Quaker Professional Services, 585 Hawthorne Ct., Galesburg, IL 61401.

It's a Dog's Life (Canine Health Care & Training), *Household Dangers, How to Keep from Losing Your Pet, No Pets Allowed* (about Finding Housing), and *Don't Panic.* Tree House Animal Foundation, 1212 West Carmen Ave., Chicago, IL 60640.

Air Travel with Pets and *Car Travel with Pets.* ASPCA Education Department, 424 E. 92nd St., New York, NY 10128.

Allergies to Animals. American Academy of Allergy & Immunology, 611 E. Wells St., Milwaukee, WI 53202.

Puppy Love: Easy Ways to Keep Your Dog Healthy and Happy. Merck, AgVet Division, P.O. Box 2000, Rahway, NJ 07065.

Traveling with Your Pet. American Veterinary Medical Association, 930 North Meacham Road, Schaumburg, IL 60196.

Keeping Your Dog Fit and Trim: A Guide to Nutrition and Exercise. American Kennel Club, 5580 Centerview Dr., Raleigh, NC 27606.

Friskies Training Manual. P.O. Box 2092, Young America, MN 55399.

Free Catalogues

The best dog book catalogue is indisputably *Direct Book Service*, which contains hundreds of dog books and tapes. Call (800) 776-2665.

The following larger catalogues contain valuable and/or entertaining items you can buy your dog:

Cherrybrook: (800) 524-0820

Discount Master Animal Care: (800) 346-0749
Doctors Foster & Smith: (800) 826-7206
J-B Wholesale Pet Supplies: (800) 526-0388
Pedigrees: (800) 548-4786
Pet Warehouse: (800) 443-1160
RC Steele: (800) 872-3773
Sam & Sally Creature Comforts: (800) 558-5859
Valley Vet Supplies: (800) 468-0059
Wholesale Pet USA: (800) 473-8872

Television Shows

We'd love to see something like an Animal Chanimal, which would be a whole channel devoted to programs mainly about domestic pets. But it will probably never happen. Considering that 60 percent of American households own either a dog or a cat, it seems amazing that there aren't more television and radio programs just for us.

We've heard (but couldn't confirm) that there is a program about dogs now in the works to be called "Canine Capers." In the meantime, you may be able to catch the following.

Dr. Jim, with Jim Humphries, D.V.M., appears on various stations.

Dr. Berney's Pet Connection, with Dr. Berney Pukay of Canada on the Discovery Channel.

The Pet Department, produced by Steve Schwartz, with host Steve Walker on the F/X Channel.

Those Incredible Animals, also on the Discovery Channel, often has a segment on dogs.

And on Radio

Animal Crackers, WCNR, Central Pennsylvania.

Talkin' Pets, with Jon Patch on Sun Radio Network, St. Petersburg, Florida.

The Pet Show, with Warren Eckstein, is on thirty stations including WOR in New York and KABC in Los Angeles.

Columns

Pet columns are wonderful sources of free information on dogs, but again, it's surprising how few of them there are out there. Some newspapers carry syndicated columns, such as the always informative "Ask Your Vet" column by Ann Huntington, which is also on Nexus, so you can look it up on a computer network if your newspaper doesn't get it. But other good columns only appear in one newspaper. If you don't live in that region, you'll never see it. Here are some columns to look for that include (or are limited to) dogs.

D'Arcy Bryan, "All About Animals," Library Features Syndicate.

Michael Capuzzo, "Wild Things," *Philadelphia Inquirer*.

Vickie Croke, "Animal Beat," *New York Times* News Service & Boston Globe.

JoAnn Davis, "Animal House," Wichita Falls *Times Record* News Service (Texas).

R.G. Elmore, "Points on Pets," Copley News Service.

Michael Fox, "Animal Doctor," United Features Syndicate.

Ranny W. Green, "Pets," *Seattle Times*.

Susan L. Hively, "Pets," *Cleveland Plain Dealer*.

Ann Huntington, D.V.M., "Ask Your Vet."

Lissa Kaplan, "Mostly About Dogs," *Dayton Daily News* (Ohio).

Frank Mainville, "Out of the Dog House," *Lansing State Journal* (Michigan).

S.A. Marcus, "Pets," *Newsday* (Long Island).

Helen Palmer, "Canine Corner," *Advocate-Messenger* (Kentucky).

"Pet Corner," (staff written), Tribune Media Services.

Gina Spadafori, "Pet Connection," Scripps-Howard News Service.

Alice Terrill, "Just Dogs," Arlington Heights, Illinois *Daily Herald*.

Computer Bulletin Boards

Most of the major bulletin boards below will allow you to try them out for a few free hours before you have to subscribe to the service. We got most of this information from *Dog Fancy*, and were unable to get too technical for you because we're only beginners on the information highway.

We're on America OnLine and Compuserve, and you can always e-mail us at paulettec@aol.com. We think we'll have learned how to reply by the time this book comes out, but if we don't respond to your e-mail, we may still be working on it. In the meantime, here are a few places you can call that have it figured out.

America Online: Pet Care Club, (800) 827-6364.

CompuServe: Pets/Animals Forum, Time Warner Dog and Cat Forum (includes Good Dog) and the Humane Society Forum, (800) 848-8199.

Delphi: Pet Lovers Forum, weekly Pet Care Conference, Opinion Polls, (800) 695-4005.

Genie: Maggie-Mae's Pet-Net & Co. Roundtable, bulletin boards, library, conferences, (800) 638-9636.

Internet: rec.pet.dogs and several related bulletin boards like rec.pet.dogs.behavior/health, etc.

Prodigy: Pets Bulletin Board, Pet Care Guide, (800) 776-3449.

Veterinary Information Network: (800) 700-4636, for veterinarians who subscribe to America Online.

How to Make Money in Dogs

The author of *How to Make Money in Dogs,* Kurt Unkelbach, had quite an entrepreneurial spirit. He pointed out that in just one hour there will be thousands more new pups in America. "Two months from now, almost as many people will start spending on those same young pups," he wrote in an old book whose ideas are still quite fresh. Here are a few of the ways he suggested that one could make money in dogs.

Book Dealer	Groomer
Behavioral Training	Handler
Breeding Dogs	Hobby Kennel
Dog Cemetery	Home Boarding
Dog Mail-Order Items	Obedience Training
Dog Outfits	Sitting
Dog Photography	Walking Dogs
Dog Therapy	Veterinarian
Dog Writing	Veterinarian's Assistant

Quiz: Are You a Dog Nut?

- Would you rather talk about your dog than your life?
- Do you refer to your dog as a child, kid, girl, or boy, and think of it as your baby or child?
- Do you carry a picture of your dog in your wallet?
- When you ask for a doggie bag in a restaurant, is it actually for him?
- Now that you've read this book, are you anxiously awaiting our next *(277 More Secrets Your Dog Wants You to Know)* so you can read even more about dogs?
- Have you ever bought things for your dog that others considered strange (jogging suit, jewelry, hats)?
- Has your dog ever affected your vacation plans?
- Do you refuse to leave home without him?
- Do you celebrate his birthday and buy a card or gifts?
- Have you ever talked to your dog on the telephone or sent him a card or postcard while you were away?
- Is your living room floor filled with doggie objects?
- Do you have jewelry or clothes or artwork with a dog on it?

If you answered yes to more than three of the above, you are a certifiable dog nut and are eligible to answer our quiz, which begins on the next page!

Quiz for Dog Nuts Only

If you took the previous quiz and qualify as a genuine dog nut, you are eligible to help us with a survey. You do not have to print your name, but you do have to send it to us or we can't use it. Use additional paper if you need it.

We regret that we will be unable to acknowledge or respond to your letters, because we are currently working on *277 More Secrets Your Dog Wants You to Know* and *277 Secrets Your Cat Wants You to Know.* Please send responses to: Paul & Paulette, P.O. Box 20474, Cherokee Station, New York, NY 10021. We'll print the results in our next dog book.

1. Do you think your dog is better looking than your spouse or significant other?

   _____

2. Do you think your dog has a better disposition than your spouse or significant other?

   _____

3. Would you rather cuddle with your dog than with your spouse or significant other?

   _____

4. Do you like your dog better than at least one of your children?

   _____

5. Whom do you trust more: your dog or your co-workers?

   _____

6. Do you (or others) think you look like your dog?

_____

7. Are you and your dog both overweight?

_____

8. Do you believe your dog will go to heaven one day?

_____

9. Do you believe your dog is psychic?

_____

10. Would you risk your life to save your dog's?

_____

11. If your dog could save the life of one hundred people you didn't know, but had to die now to do it, what would you do?

_____

12. If your dog was dying, and there was an experimental treatment that would cost you every cent you have and force you to mortgage your house, would you do it?

_____

13. If you had a chance to live in much better housing for the same amount of money but it meant giving up your dog, would you?

_____

Thank you for your help!

Additional References

Most of the sources are listed directly in each chapter, but here are a few more for the chapters indicated. For full citations on the books mentioned below, see Suggested Reading (and Viewing) About Dogs (page 181).

Embarrassing Habits of Your Dog...

Mondo Canine/Dog World/Bottom Line/McCall's/Pets and Your Health

Do Dogs Cause Multiple Sclerosis?

Medical Reports

Anderson, Larry J., M.D.; Robert F. Kibler, M.D.; Richard A. Kaslow, M.D.; Jobie Austin, B.A.; and Robert C. Holman, M.S. "Multiple Sclerosis Unrelated to Dog Exposure." *Neurology,* vol. 34 (Sept. 1984).

Bauer, H.J., and J. Wikstrom. "Multiple Sclerosis and House Pets." [letter] *The Lancet* (Nov. 12, 1977).

Cook, Stuart D., M.D.; Benjamin H. Natelson, M.D.; Barry E. Levin, M.D.; Pamela S. Chavis, M.D.; and Peter C. Dowling, M.D. "Further Evidence of a Possible Association between House Dogs and Multiple Sclerosis." *Annals of Neurology,* vol. 3 (2), Feb. 1978.

Cook, Stuart D., M.D., and Peter C. Dowling, M.D. "A Possible Association between House Pets and Multiple Sclerosis." *The Lancet* (May 7, 1977).

Cook, Stuart, M.D., and Peter C. Dowling, M.D. "Distemper and Multiple Sclerosis in Sitka, Alaska." *Annals of Neurology,* vol. 11 (2), Feb. 1982.

Cook, Stuart D., M.D., and Peter C. Dowling, M.D. "Multiple Sclerosis and Viruses: An Overview." *Neurology,* vol. 30, no. 2 (July 1980).

Cook, S.D., B. Blumberg, P.C. Dowling, W. Deans, and R. Cross. "Multiple Sclerosis and Canine Distemper on Key West, Florida." [letter] *The Lancet* (June 20, 1987).

Cook, Stuart D., M.D., Benjamin Blumberg, Ph.D., and Peter C. Dowling, M.D. "Potential Role of Paramyxoviruses in Multiple Sclerosis." *Neurologic Clinics,* vol. 4, no. 1 (Feb. 1986).

Cook, S.D., P.C. Dowling, J. Norman, and S. Jablon. "Multiple Sclerosis and Canine Distemper in Iceland." [letter] *The Lancet* (Feb. 17, 1979).

Cook, S.D., P.C. Dowling, and W.C. Russell. "Multiple Sclerosis and Canine Distemper." [letter] *The Lancet* (March 18, 1978).

Krakowka, Steven, D.V.M., Ph.D.; James A. Miele, M.S.; Lawrence E. Mathes, Ph.D.; and Alfred E. Metzler, Dr. Med. Vet. "Antibody Responses to Measles Virus and Canine Distemper Virus in Multiple Sclerosis." *Annals of Neurology,* vol. 14, no. 5 (Nov. 1983).

Landtblom, A.M.; U. Flodin; M. Karlsson; S. Palhagen; O. Axelson; B. Soderfeldt. "Multiple Sclerosis and Exposure to Solvents, Ionizing Radiation and Animals." [abstract] *Scandinavian Journal of Work, Environment, and Health,* vol. 19, no. 6 (Dec. 1993).

Madden, David L., D.V.M., Ph.D.; William C. Wallen, Ph.D.; Sidney A. Houff, M.D.; Isabel C. Shekarchi, Ph.D.; Pauli O. Leinikki, M.D., Ph.D.; Gabriel A. Castellano, Ph.D.; and John L. Sever, M.D., Ph.D. "Measles and Canine Distemper Antibody: Presence in Sera from Patients with Multiple Sclerosis and Matched Control Subjects." *Archives of Neurology,* vol. 38 (Jan. 1981).

Nathanson, Neal, Pall A. Palsson, and Gunnar Gudmundsson. "Multiple Sclerosis and Canine Distemper in Iceland." *The Lancet* (Nov. 25, 1978).

Norman, James E., Jr., Ph.D.; Stuart D. Cook, M.D.; and Peter C. Dowling, M.D. "Household Pets Among Veterans with Multiple Sclerosis and Age-Matched Controls, Pilot Survey." *Archives of Neurology,* vol. 40 (April 1983).

Poskanzer, David C., L. Bradford Prenney, and Jean L. Sheridan. "House Pets and Multiple Sclerosis." [letter] *The Lancet* (June 4, 1977).

Read, David, Delia Nassim, Peter Smith, Chris Patterson, and Charles Warlow. "Multiple Sclerosis and Dog Ownership: A Case-Control Investigation." *Journal of the Neurological Sciences,* vol. 55 (1982).

Stephenson, John R., Volker Ter Meulen, and Wolfgang Kiessling. "Search for Canine-Distemper Virus Antibodies in Multiple Sclerosis, a Detailed Virological Evaluation." *The Lancet* (Oct. 11, 1980).

Sullivan, Constance B., DrPH; Barbara R. Visscher, M.D., DrPH; and Roger Detels, M.D., M.S. "Multiple Sclerosis and Age at Exposure to Childhood Diseases and Animals: Cases and Their Friends. *Neurology,* vol. 34 (Sept. 1984).

Newspaper Articles

Cheakalos, Christina. "MS Victims Want Results of State Studies." *Miami Herald,* Feb. 21, 1988.

Ornstein, Susan. "MS Scare at Hospital Raised in Buy-Out Talks." *Miami Herald,* April 24, 1986.

Sternberg, Steve. "MS Research Points to a Mystery Infection/Key West Clues Challenge Beliefs About Disease." *Miami Herald,* Nov. 10, 1985.

21 Spots Your Dog Loves to Have...Massaged
Mondo Canine/Dogwatching

Are Some Dogs Psychic?
The A to Z Guide to Dogs/McCalls

The O.J. Simpson Case...
Good Dog!

90 Little-Known Dangers That Could Harm Your Dog
Special thanks to Dr. Ernest Poortinga for checking this chapter. Material

comes from *Dog World/American Journal/New York Post/Daily News/Good Dog/Dog Fancy/Ask Your Vet/Bottom Line*/American Humane Society/*Cornell University Animal Health Newsletter/Dr. Edell's Healthletter/Your Health/Mondo Canine/Newsday/Parents/Animal Behaviour Consultant Newsletter/125 Most Often Asked Questions About Dogs/Kennel Healthline*.

How to Teach Your Dog to Sing...
Dogs Today

60 Diseases You Can Catch from Your Dog...
Our thanks also to Dr. James B. Miller for going through this complicated chapter.

9 "People" Foods You Should Never Feed Your Dog
Good Dog!/Newsday/Dr. Edell's Healthletter

How to Tell What Your Dog Is Thinking by Looking at His Tail...
Animals for the Performing Arts (APA)/*How to Get Your Dog to Do What You Want/The Intelligence of Dogs/How to Talk to Your Dog/Mondo Canine/Dog World*

Would Prozac Help Your Dog?
Your Health/Good Morning America

Questions Most Often Asked of "Dog Lawyers"
Dog World

What Your Dog Can Hear, Smell, and See...
Dogwatching/Dog Problems: The Gentle Modern Cure/Teach Your Dog to Behave/Wild About Animals

How to Keep the Airlines from Killing Your Dog
Ask the Vet/Dog Fancy

How Dogs Track Drugs...
Good Dog!

How to Give Your Dog Pills...
Dog Fancy/Dog World/"Your Dog's Teeth" (from Purina)

How to Find Your Missing Dog...
Dog Fancy

How to Use Your Dog's Hair to Make a Sweater
Good Dog!

Why Christmas May Not Be So Merry for Your Dog
*Good Dog!/Animals' Agenda/*Tufts University School of Veterinary Medicine's *Your Dog* newsletter

16 Secrets to Help You Pick Your Next Puppy
Dog Facts

Vacationing with Your Dog...
Dog World/DogGone/Dog Fancy

Plants That Can Poison Your Dog
National Animal Poison Control Center/*The Kennel Doctor/KennelHealthline*

The 50 Words Your Dog May Know...
To compile the list of fifty words, people with dogs were given a list of one hundred words from *Your Pet's Secret Language*. Respondents were asked to check off any words their dogs understood, and to write in any special words their dogs responded to that were not included in the list. Thanks to Remi and Alicen Harrad and Francesca David for assisting with the questionnaire.

How to Give Your Dog a Nose-to-Toes Examination
Pukay, Dr. Barney, "Pet Connection"

18 (Mostly Free) Hotlines...
Free Stuff for Your Pet/Dog Fancy/Dog World

Sidebark Additional References

The Real Reasons Dogs Lick Us: *Superdog*

Robert Browning Loved Elizabeth Barrett Browning, But Not Her Dog: *Good Dog!*

Pampered Pets of Japan: *National Enquirer*

Is Your Pet Better Looking Than Your Spouse?: *Harper* Index

The Richest Dogs on Record: *Mondo Canine/First Pet History of the World*

Wear White Socks to Find Out If Your Dog Has Fleas: *Bottom Line*

Fascinating Facts about Fleas: *PetDogs*

Bet Your Dog Can't Do This!: *Dog Fancy/First Pet History of the World*

Are Rawhide Chews Effective—and Safe?: *Dog World*

Simple Trick Stops Dogs from Biting: *Dog World*

Suggested Reading
(and Viewing) about Dogs

The following books, articles and newsletters were all sources for this book and we acknowledge the authors, editors, producers, and publishers for their information.

Bamberger, Michelle, D.V.M. *Help! The Quick Guide to First Aid for Your Dog.* New York: Howell Book House, 1993.

Barrie, Anmarie, Esq. *Dogs and the Law.* Neptune City, NJ: T.F.H. Publications, Inc.

Benjamin, Carol Lea. *Second-Hand Dog: How To Turn Yours Into a First-Rate Pet.* New York: Howell Book House, 1988.

Bowman, Linda. *Free Stuff for Your Pet.* Chicago: Probus Publishing Company, 1992.

Bulanda, Susan. *The Canine Source Book 4th Edition: Almost Everything You Wanted to Know About Dogs.* Portland, OR: Doral Publishing, 1994.

Cahill, Kevin M., M.D., and William O'Brien, M.D. *Pets and Your Health: Living Safely with Animals.* London, England: Kingswood Press, 1987.

Caras, Roger. *A Dog Is Listening.* New York: Simon & Schuster, 1993.

Comfort, David. *The First Pet History of the World.* New York: Fireside, 1994.

Condax, Kate Delano. *101 Training Tips for Your Dog.* New York: Dell, 1994.

Coren, Stanley. *The Intelligence of Dogs: Canine Consciousness and Capabilities.* New York: Free Press/Macmillan, 1994.

Crolius, Kendall, and Anne Montgomery. *Knitting with Dog Hair: A Woof-to-Warp Guide to Making Hats, Sweaters, Mittens and Much More.* New York: St. Martin's Press, 1994.

Denenberg, R.V. *The Dog Catalog.* New York: Grosset & Dunlap, 1978.

Dibra, Bashkim, with Elizabeth Randolph. *Teach Your Dog to Behave.* New York: Dutton, 1993.

Eckstein, Warren, with Andrea Eckstein. *How to Get Your Dog to Do What You Want.* New York: Fawcett Columbine/Ballantine Books, 1994.

Fogle, Bruce, *101 Questions Your Dog Would Ask Its Vet If Your Dog Could Talk.* New York: Tetra Press, 1993

Fogle, Bruce, D.V.M., M.R.C.V.S. *The Dog's Mind: Understanding Your Dog's Behavior.* New York: Howell Book House, 1990.

Fox, Michael W. *Dr. Michael Fox's Massage Program for Cats and Dogs.* New York: Newmarket Press, 1981.

Fox, Dr. Michael W. *Superdog: Raising the Perfect Canine Companion.* New York: Howell Book House, 1990.

Fraser, Clarence M., D.V.M., editor. *The Merck Veterinary Manual.* Merck & Co., 1991.

Gellman, Rabbi Marc, and Monsignor Thomas Hartman. *Where Does God Live? Questions and Answers for Parents and Children.* Liguori, MO: Triumph Books, 1991.

George, Jean Craighead. *How to Talk to Your Dog.* New York: Warner, 1985.

Green, Martin I. *The Home Pet Vet Guide for Dogs.* New York: Ballantine, 1980.

Haggerty, Captain Arthur J., and Carol Lea Benjamin. *Dog Tricks: Teaching Your Dog to Be Useful, Fun and Entertaining.* New York: Howell Book House, 1978.

Hamer, Lynne M. *Name That Dog.* West Chester, PA: Animal Press, 1994. (700 W. Downington Pike, 105-139, West Chester, PA 19380; $24.95.)

Kay, William, D.V.M., with Elizabeth Randolph. *The Complete Book of Dog Health.* New York: Macmillan, 1985.

Malone, John. *The 125 Most Asked Questions About Dogs.* New York: William Morrow, 1993.

Marder, Amy, V.M.D. *Your Healthy Pet: A Practical Guide to Choosing and Raising Happier, Healthier Dogs and Cats.* Emmaus, PA: Rodale, 1994.

Mezo, Nicole, C.M.T. *On Cloud K-9: How to Massage Your Dog.* Stinson Beach, CA: del sol Press, 1993. (P.O. Box 244, Stinson Beach, CA 94970; $8.95, plus $1.10 for postage.)

Monks of New Skete. *How to Be Your Dog's Best Friend: A Training Manual for Dog Owners.* Boston: Little, Brown and Co., 1978.

Morris, Desmond. *Dogwatching.* New York: Crown, 1986.

Neville, Peter. *Pet Sex: The Rude Facts of Life for the Family Dog, Cat and Rabbit.* England: Sidgwick & Jackson Limited, 1993. (Available from Peter Neville for $20 at 4 Quarry Cottages, Chicksgrove Tisbury Salsbury Wiltshire SP3 6LZ ENGLAND.)

Palmer, Joan. *Dog Facts.* New York: Barnes & Noble, 1993.

Radbill, Dr. Steven, with Morris Kennedy. *The Complete Book of Questions Dog Owners Ask Their Vet & Answers.* Philadelphia: Running Press, 1980.

Randolph, Mary. *Dog Law.* Berkeley, CA: Nolo Press, 1994.

Robbins, Jhan. *Your Pet's Secret Language.* New York: Peter H. Wyden, 1975.

Siegal, Mordecai, and Matthew Margolis. *Good Dog, Bad Dog: Dog Training Made Easy.* New York: Henry Holt, 1991.

Smith, Scott S. *Pet Souls: Evidence That Animals Survive Death.* Thousand Oaks, CA: Light Source Research, 1994. (2455 Calle Roble, Thousand Oaks, CA 91360; $13.95, plus $2.00 for postage and handling.)

Smythe, R.H., M.R.C.V.S. *The Private Life of the Dog.* New York: Arco, 1965.

Thomas, Dawn Curie, D.V.M., and William S. Thomas. *Ask The Vet.* Santa Barbara, CA: Veterinarian's Best, 1993. (Veterinarian's Best, Inc., P.O. Box 4459, Santa Barbara, CA 93103; $7.95, plus $2.00 for postage.)

Unkelbach, Kurt. *How to Make Money in Dogs.* New York: Dodd, Mead & Co, 1974.

Walker, Liz, John Haynsworth, and Bonnie Skinner Levy. *Top Dog: Canines and Their Companions.* Wilsonville, OR: Beautiful America Publishing Co., 1991.

Weitzman, Nan, and Ross Becker. *The Dog Food Book.* Charleston, SC: Good Dog, 1994. (P.O. Box 10069, Austin, TX 78766; $11.95)

Weston, David, and Ruth Ross. *Dog Problems: The Gentle Modern Cure.* New York: Howell Book House, 1992.

Whitney, Leon F., D.V.M., and George D. Whitney, D.V.M. *The Complete Book of Dog Care.* rev. ed. New York: Doubleday, 1985.

Winokur, Jon. *Mondo Canine.* New York: Dutton, 1992.

Wood, Gerald L. *Guinness Book of Pet Records.* London, England: Guinness Superlatives Ltd., 1984.

Woodhouse, Barbara. *The A to Z Guide to Dogs.* New York: Stein & Day, 1972.

Videotapes

Cornwell, Michael J., D.V.M. "Safety Is Fun." (Glencoe Animal Hospital, 3712 N. High St., Columbus, OH 43214; $49.95.)

Harry, M.W., D.V.M. "How You Can Help Save Your Dog's Life." (Sonoma Video Productions, Santa Rosa, CA.)

Kilcommons, Brian. "Good Owners, Great Dogs: How to Make Dog Training Easy and Fun." (The Family Dog, RD 2 Box 398 Prospect Rd., Middletown, NY 10947; $19.95, plus $3.95 postage. 1-800-457-PETS.)

Additional Recommendations
(not used in this book)

Photography book: Freedman, Jill. *Jill's Dogs.* Rohnert Park, CA: Pomegranate Artbooks, 1993. (Duotone photographs of working dogs; magnificent and moving, like all of her photographs.)

Audiotape: Routledge, Ric. "Dog Talk." Weekly tapes for breeders and exhibitors, which are intended to be played in their car while going to shows. (Contact American Dog, P.O. Box 127, Montepelier, IN 47359; $150 for 50 tapes.)

NOTE: We listed purchasing information when current books or tapes might be difficult to obtain. All the rest of the current books are available in your local bookstore, or at specialized book sources like Dog Lovers Bookshop in New York (at 9 West 31st Street) and the Pirhana Shop in Toronto, or from Direct Book Service at (800) 776-2665.

Some of the older books listed above may show up from time to time at back date dog book companies, such as Carol Butcher, the Complete Dog Story, and Tarmans Books. All are excellent, but we especially recommend Tarmans Books, 10 Dunover Ct., P.O. Box E, Hummelstown, PA 17036.

Large American Magazines
for the Dog Lover

Dog Fancy
P.O. Box 53264
Boulder, CO 80322
(800) 365-4421
They also publish *Dogs U.S.A.*

Dog World
Intertec Publishing Corp.
29 North Wacker Dr.
Chicago, IL 60606
(800) 361-8056

Good Dog!
P.O. Box 10069
Austin, TX 78766
(800) 968-1738

AKC Gazette
51 Madison Ave.
New York, NY, 10010
(919) 233-9769

There are many excellent magazines we examined but did not have space to list, including regional publications (such as *Pethouse* in New York, *Pet Times* in Chicago, the *Canine Classified* in Houston, the *Cold Nose Chronicle* in Missouri, and the *Central Ohio Canine Press*).

There are also many wonderful small general publications (such as *Best Friends* magazines), publications for special interests (like *Natural Pet* magazine), and breed publications (like *The Corgi Cryer*). For an expanded list of available publications, consult *The Canine Source Book*, by Susan Bulanda.

Magazines Published Outside
of the United States

All accept subscriptions from America.

Dogs in Canada
Apex Dog Publisher
89 Skyway Ave.
Etobicoke ONT M9W 6R4
(Note: their annual edition is
   especially good.)

Dogs Today
Pet Subjects Limited
6 Station Parade
Sunningdale, Berkshire,
5L5 OPE England

Pet Dogs
P.O. Box 163
Huddersfield, HD4 7YZ England

Wild About Animals
40 Grays Inn Rd.
WC1X 8LR England

Newsletters

Cornell University Animal Health Newsletter
P.O. Box 52816
Boulder, CO 80321

DogGone
P.O. Box 651155
Austin, TX 78766

Dog Industry Newsletter
P.O. Box 10096
Austin, TX 78766

People, Pets & Vets
P.O. Box 26251
Phoenix, AZ 85068

The Scoop
17825 Meridian Rd.
Elbert, CO 80106

Your Dog
Tufts University School of
Veterinary Medicine
203 Harrison Ave.
Boston, MA 02111

A Dog's Life

While you were reading this book, as many as two thousand dogs may have been put to sleep in shelters throughout the United States because no one wanted them, or could take them, and/or there wasn't enough money for the shelters to care for them.

As many as one thousand of those dogs may have once lived in a house and been someone's adored pet, just like yours.

Coming Soon in
277 More Secrets Your Dog
Wants You to Know

More Embarrassing Habits of Your Dogs...More Little-Known Hazards...Unusual and Expensive Gifts...Celebrities and Their Dogs...Free Items You Can Get...How to Save Money on Heartworm Medication...Simple Japanese Technique That Reduces a Dog's Bark to ⅒ the Sound...Dog Foods That Have the Lowest Fat and Calories...Dangers of the Lyme Disease Vaccine...New Age Dogs...Dog Sex...How to Spot the Signs of Cancer, Heart Disease, and Three Other Illnesses That Could Kill Your Dog...The Death of a Dog Can Hurt More Than the Death of a Parent...Seven Ways to Housebreak Your Dog by Next Week—Even If He's Older...How to Handle Your Dog's Five Biggest Fears...Vaccinating Your Own Dogs to Save Money...Handling People Emotions in Dogs (Depression, Jealousy, Stress)...Dogs Are Smarter Than You Think...How to Tell a Dog's Age from His Teeth...Plastic Surgery for Your Dog...Dog Sleep...Battered Dogs...Questions Most Often Asked of Dog Behaviorists...Do Flea Collars Work?...The Best Flea Remedies Available...How to Make Your White Dog Look Like a Panda...How to Collect a Urine Sample...Dogs and Your Garden...How to Save Your Dog in Any Emergency...Could Your Dog Win at Westminster?...How Much Is Your Dog Like a Wolf?...Should You Debark Your Dog?...The Five Biggest Causes of Accidental Dog Poisoning and How to Protect Your Pet...Everything You Need to Know about Pet Insurance...Avoiding a Bout with Bloat...Why You Shouldn't Feel Guilty If You Don't Brush Your Dog's Teeth...And Much, Much More!

Index

C

Cabot, Susan, 29

Canine Good Citizen Test, 51, 158–59

Caras, Roger, 22–23, 77

Careers, 173

Carpenter, Sherry, 32, 158–59

Cars, dogs in, 43–44, 49, 51

Catalogues, 169–70

Cataracts, 142

Cat population, 129

Cat scratch disease, 2

Cawley, Linda, 83–84

Celebrities' dogs, 101–4

Chihuahuas, 88

Children: avoiding dog bites, 51–52, 86–88; catching diseases from dogs, 57, 59; dog books for, 50; licked by dogs, 2–3

Chocolate, 60

Choking, 24–25

Chow chows, 88, 100, 130, 151

Christmas, 136–37

Cocker spaniels, 103

Collars: dangerous, 43; electronic flea, 71; safety, 50; shock, 25

Collies, 88, 122, 141

Companion Animal Geriatric Center, 155

Computer bulletin boards, 172

Condax, Kate Delano, 96, 119

Constantino, Vinnie, 127

Cook, Stuart D., 15

Cooper, Jan, 14

Coren, Stanley, 68, 79, 151

Cornwell, J. Michael, 86–87, 135

Corwin, Lisa, 19

Crime, 13, 117–18

Crolius, Kendall, 125

Crufts Dog Show, 12

Crystals, 27

Cuddy, Beverly, 12

D

Dachshunds, 35, 103, 161

Dalmatians, 34–35, 66, 103, 130, 141

Death: of dogs, 83–84, 165–66; of owners, 48, 153–55

Depression, 74–75

Diapers, 46

Dibra, Bashkim, 4

Dieting, 131–32

Diseases: communicated by licking, 1–4; most prevalent, 123–24; passed from dogs to humans, 15–18, 56–59; passed from humans to dogs, 56; venereal, 7

Distemper, 16–18

Doberman pinschers, 128, 151

Dog shows, 12–13

Drug-sniffing dogs, 12–13, 111–12

Dunbar, Ian, 68

E

Eastwood, Abe, 17–18

Eckstein, Warren, 68, 78, 152

Empel, Jay, 97

L

Labrador retrievers, 103, 122, 128, 151

Ladalia, Kathleen, 111

Lamb, Rachel, 154

L-deprenyl, 10–11

Legal questions, 83–85, 154–55

Letterman, David, 33–36, 109–10

Licking, 1–4

Life vests, 50–51

Lost dogs, 117–21, 165

M

Mandelberger, Fanny, 19

Marder, Amy, 156

Margolis, Matthew, 79, 112

Marijuana, 61

Marks, Dennis, 109

Marriages, dogs and, 30

Massages, 19–23

McGuire, Malise, 125

Medical care: five-minute examination, 156–57; hotlines for, 164–65; reasons for, 157

Medication, giving, 113–15

Mezo, Nicole, 19

Milgram, Bill, 10–11

Miller, James B., 1–4, 56, 87

Mirrors, 90

Molay, Richard, 136–37

Montgomery, Ann, 125

Morris, Desmond, 6–7, 27, 68, 90

Mounting, 7–8, 70

Movies, 63–66

Multiple sclerosis, 15–18

N

National Dog Registry, 120

Neutering, 165

Neville, Peter, 8

Newspaper columns, 171–72

O

Obedience class, 14

O'Brien, Dennis, 75

Onions, 60

P

Pampering, 2, 70–73, 75

Paper-training, 139

Papillons, 151

Patterson, Wes, 31

Pekingese, 100

Personal ads, 78

Phillips, Florence, 120–21

Photographs, publication of, 34

Pit bulls, 38, 88, 128, 133, 161

Plants, poisonous, 146–48

Plechner, Alfred J., 97

Pomeranians, 103

Poodles, 88, 103, 129, 151

Poortinga, Ernest, 60–62

Population, dog, 129, 145

Products: expensive, 93–95; safety, 48–53; unusual, 70–73

Prozac, 74–75

Pseudomonas infections, 4

Psychic powers, 26–28, 70

Pugs, 3

Puppies, 138–40

Tuberculosis, 3
Tyler, Ann, 77

U
Unkelbach, Kurt, 173

V
Vacation spots, 143–44
Vacuum cleaners, 126
Venereal diseases, 7
Vision, 91–92
Vocabularies, 149–51

W
Walsh, John C., 160–62
Wecht, Cyril, 31
Weston, Ruth, 8
Whitney, George D., 4, 56,
    133–34
Wills. *See* Legal questions
Woodhouse, Barbara, 20, 26, 68

Y
Yorkshire terriers, 103